Hotels, Motels & Inns of Florida

Kristen Hare

Reedy Press
PO Box 5131
St. Louis, MO 63139
reedypress.com

Library of Congress Control Number: 2024939007
ISBN: 9781681064796

Unless otherwise indicated, all photos are courtesy of the author or in the public domain.

Printed in the United States of America
24 25 26 27 28   5 4 3 2 1

Dedication

For Bonnie, who made me a traveler and traveled with me to many of these special spots.

Courtesy of The Colony Hotel

CONTENTS

ACKNOWLEDGMENTS

Thank you to everyone at the hotels, motels, and inns I visited and reached out to for this book. They took my calls, offered tours, shared old and new images, rummaged through postcards and brochures, and told the stories and histories of their establishments. Thank you to the local, state, and national historians who helped put these places in the context of time and space. I'm particularly grateful for the treasure chest of archives at Florida Memory from the State Library and Archives of Florida. The reporting in this book was deeply enriched thanks to area libraries and historical centers and societies. Thanks to my friends and family who joined me on visits. A good part of this book wouldn't exist without generations of work from local journalists and newspapers. Thank you to Marriott International and Tarpon Lodge for offering stays at several properties featured in this book.

I also want to acknowledge the people who lived in Florida before it was Florida. Before the railroads and pirates and European explorers, Florida was home to diverse and thriving communities of Indigenous people, including the Timucua, Calusa, and the many people who came after them. Today, Florida is home to the Seminole, Poarch Creek, and Miccosukee tribes.

Vinoy, Courtesy of Marriott International

Courtesy of Gasparilla Inn

Introduction

This book started with an obituary I wrote for the *Tampa Bay Times*. When Willie Robinson Jr. died in 2019, I learned of his life's work preserving the Jackson House, his family's home in what was the Scrub neighborhood of Tampa. Robinson's grandparents turned their home into a rooming house that hosted Black travelers for decades. One year later, I wrote an obituary about a woman behind another Tampa Bay landmark. This one was for Mary Falkenstein, known to all as Nanny, who ran the Keystone Motel on Pass-a-Grille Beach. One of Nanny's wise sayings included calling clear days "postcard perfect."

These stories got me thinking. I wanted to know more about the places where generations of tourists have stayed and generations of families have maintained.

And if there's one thing I've learned about the place the rest of the world vacations, it's that there's always something else worth exploring. In the three editions of my book *100 Things to Do in Tampa Bay Before You Die*, I've worked through bucket lists of adventures. And I've stuck to my motto since I moved to Florida: don't let the tourists have all the fun.

But there's still one category that tourists relish and locals rarely think about—our hotels, motels, and inns.

Despite this Airbnb era where you can live like a local with your own kitchen and bedroom, Florida maintains excellent hotels, motels, and inns.

And the historic ones have some fascinating stories to tell.

One man's ashes rest in the window planter of a motel overlooking the Gulf of Mexico. Al Capone's name haunts many places I visited with stories of hidden tunnels. Florida's inns and lodges have hosted movie stars and starred in movies. And year after year, people return to the places they visited as children, now with their own children and grandchildren, hoping for their favorite rooms.

It's a living history for a nightly rate.

Across the state, you'll find historic properties that each tell a story about Florida: Gilded Age palaces built for new railroad passengers in the late 1800s and early 1900s; grand pink hotels of the 1920s; mom-and-pop spots that sprung up in the 1930s and '40s; quirky motels of the 1950s and '60s; and fantastical hotels Walt Disney built for his brand-new theme park in the 1970s.

This book features a few more than 60 of them—hotels, motels, and inns that are still open and that are 50 years old or older. The majority are on the National Register of Historic Places. Many are recognized by the Historic Hotels of America. While reporting, I found at least another 40 hotels, motels, and inns that aren't included, though not for lack of trying.

You'll also find a section on Florida's historic Black-owned hotels, which, like the Jackson House, were established when segregation prevented Black travelers from staying at and enjoying many of Florida's wonders. I didn't get to every single one, including a notable handful such as the Campbell Hotel in Daytona Beach, the Colson House in Sarasota, LaFrance in DelRay, Wells'Built in Orlando, and the Dunbar in Gainesville. Each of them, whether in this book or not, shows entrepreneurship, resistance, and joy that deserve to be recognized and remembered.

And because Florida is still Florida, I've included five special spots at the end that aren't historic hotels exactly but will certainly go down as special in many people's personal histories. They include examples of adaptive reuse at an old courthouse, schoolhouse, and cigar factory, and newer wonders including pyramids and a giant guitar.

I should warn you that I mostly stayed away from the ghosts that haunt some of these spots, though I loved hearing their stories. Many,

many of the places I visited and reported on were happy to share the cold spots and light flares and the unexplained. I simply found the documented histories of the people and places in this book more fascinating than our friends on the other side.

Finally, this book includes a lot of the gorgeous historic postcards I found through my travels and reporting. They strike me as a pre-internet social media created specifically to cultivate FOMO. Imagine freezing in some northern state and getting a "Greetings From" postcard from your snooty sister in the sun. It's delicious. For those postcards in the public domain, I've made copies, so if you'd like to have one, email oldfloridahotels@gmail.com, and I'll do my best to send you a little piece of the past.

Wish you were here,

Kristen Hare

LATE 1800s

Florida's exoticness was key to the state's early hold on Americans' imaginations. There were jungles. Dangerous beasts. Beautiful birds. And so much sunshine.

And by the late 1800s, there was money to be spent here.

"This was the Gilded Age, this was the Industrial Revolution, so you had an immense amount of wealth going to a small amount of businesses and industrial tycoons," said Florida historian Joseph Vars.

After the Civil War, those tycoons saw potential in Florida. They built railroad lines and the commerce up around them.

"To drum up business for the rail lines and commercial sector and to further conspicuous consumption, they started building these pleasure palaces down in Florida," Vars said. "Florida was this great open canvas."

And, because they'd already built summer resorts in the North, they knew what they were doing.

The hotels built for the railroads "in a large part created the image of Florida and the towns that they were in," said Rodney Kite-Powell, director of the Touchton Map Library and Florida Center for Cartographic Education at the Tampa Bay History Center.

This era, Vars said, "was the foundation that the rest of Florida's tourist industry was built on."

Florida House Inn

Fernandina Beach

Opened: 1857 | Rooms: 17

What makes it special: In its long history, this inn has hosted soldiers, presidents, revolutionaries, and socialities.

The Florida House Inn opened, as near as historians can tell, between 1857 and 1859 and was soon used to house Union soldiers during the Civil War, according to the Amelia Island Museum of History. By 1873, Annie Leddy took over the inn and it became the place to stay, including by President "Ulysses S. Grant, José Marti, the Rockefellers and the Carnegies," according to 1991 reporting from the *South Florida Sun Sentinel.* Leddy was a force. "It was unheard of, in that time, for a woman to not only own property but to run a business outside of her husband's interests," the hotel's website reads. Leddy died in 1908 and her daughter continued running the property for years. Leddy's obituary, in the *Fernandina Record,* remembered her as "one of Fernandina's oldest and most highly esteemed women." Leddy's daughter sold the property in 1940, and the inn became a boarding house. Over time, the property started deteriorating. In 1990, it was rescued by new owners and has had many since then. It is included on the National Register of Historic Places. Thought to be the state's oldest hotel, the Florida House Inn is also home to the restaurant Leddy's Porch, named after the remarkable woman who put the Florida House Inn on the map.

If you visit: Head to nearby Cumberland Island to see the wild horses.

22 S 3rd St.
Fernandina Beach, Florida 32034

floridahouse.com

Courtesy of Joseph Vars

Top left and right: Courtesy of Kristen Hare. *Middle and bottom:* Courtesy of Island Hotel

ISLAND HOTEL

CEDAR KEY

OPENED: 1859 | ROOMS: 10

WHAT MAKES IT SPECIAL: THIS TINY HOTEL STARTED AS A GENERAL STORE IN THE MID-1800S.

Cedar Key's Island Hotel has been the backdrop for quite a bit of history. Made of limestone, oyster shells, and sand, it survived two hurricanes, one in 1896 and the other in 1950. Built originally as a general store between 1859 and 1860, the building is thought to have housed both Confederate and Union soldiers at different times during the Civil War. By the late 1800s, it opened to guests, and in 1915, Parson and Hale's General Store officially was converted into a hotel. The hotel has had several owners, including one who is rumored to have run it as something of a bordello in the 1930s, according to the hotel's accounting of history. The iconic mural of Neptune in the Neptune Lounge and Bar was added in 1948. In 1949, Bessy and "Gibby" Gibbs took over, cleaning things up and renaming the landmark Island Hotel. Jimmy Buffett reportedly visited the hotel in the '80s and performed in the bar. In 2002, the owners fired all staff and closed the hotel, but in 2004 Andy and Stanley Bair stepped in and revived the old spot.

IF YOU VISIT: STOP BY THE HOTEL'S NEPTUNE LOUNGE AND BAR FOR A COOL DRINK AND A GOOD LOOK AT THAT MURAL.

373 2ND ST.
CEDAR KEY, FLORIDA 32625

islandhotel-cedarkey.com

Lakeside Inn

Mount Dora

Opened: 1883 | Rooms: 90

What makes it special: Visit for a drink or meal on the lakefront veranda.

This sprawling spot opened in 1883 as a 10-room hotel called the Alexander House. In 1893, it was sold by the community members who built it and the new owner, Emma Boone, named it the Lake House. "In 1886, the Sanford and Lake Eustis Railroad was completed through Mount Dora, and a winter Chautauqua campground was established nearby," according to the nomination form for the National Register of Historic Places. "These events assured a steady and substantial flow of tourists, and the fact that the railroad depot was located just across the tracks from the Lake House undoubtedly contributed to the success of the hotel." When she married in 1903, Boone renamed it again, this time to the name that would stick—Lakeside Inn. Throughout the early 1900s, additions expanded the hotel's footprint and the number of guests it could hold. In January of 1930, former President Calvin Coolidge and his wife, Grace, helped open the hotel for the season to a crowd of 10,000, according to news clippings from the time. The inn had different owners in the mid-1900s, and in 1985 it was slated for demolition when a new buyer stepped in to renovate the property. Five years later, it went into foreclosure and was sold at auction. Since 2010, current owners Jim and Alexandra Gunderson have cared for the special spot.

If you visit: Mount Dora has streets of great restaurants and shopping with antiques, boutiques, and everything in between.

**100 N Alexander St.
Mount Dora, Florida 32757**

lakeside-inn.com

Top right and bottom left: Courtesy of Kristen Hare. *All others:* Courtesy of State Library and Archives of Florida 1910, 1940

Bottom left: Courtesy of State Library and Archives of Florida
All others: Courtesy of Marriott International

Casa Monica Resort & Spa

St. Augustine

Opened: 1888 | Rooms: 138

What makes it special: This Spanish-Moorish palace is still a thing to behold.

Casa Monica was not built by the railroad magnates who constructed trains, railways, and grand hotels for people to visit. But it was rescued by one. The hotel was built by Franklin Smith, who was predicted to be remembered for the Spanish-Moorish palace. "Long after his mortal part shall have been gathered to mother earth, the structures he has erected in St. Augustine will remain as living monuments to his art and taste and liberality," read a rather glowing dispatch from Palatka's *Daily News* in January of 1888. A few months later, stretched dangerously with the expensive enterprise, Smith sold the hotel to Henry Flagler, according to Historic Hotels of America. Flagler, the railroad magnate who built the Hotel Ponce de Leon and Alcazar Hotel in St. Augustine, soon renamed the Casa Monica the Cordova Hotel. The Alcazar and the Cordova eventually were connected, and when the Alcazar struggled and closed in the 1930s, the Cordova did, too. The Alcazar became the Lightner Museum in 1948; the Ponce de Leon closed in 1967 and became Flagler College one year later. After 30 years of sitting mostly empty, Casa Monica became the county courthouse. In 2000, the building was renovated and reopened as a hotel with its original name. In 2010, the hotel was the first to become part of the Autograph Collection from Marriott International. People might not know Franklin Smith's name these days, but the hotel he built is certainly still a living monument.

If you visit: Head to the St. Augustine Lighthouse and climb to the top. The views are worth it.

95 Cordova St.
St. Augustine, Florida 32084
marriott.com

Island Inn

Sanibel Island

Opened: 1895 | Rooms: After Hurricane Ian, 20

What makes it special: If you love shells, Sanibel is the place to be, and the inn here hosted the island's first-ever shell show.

When Will and Harriett "Granny" Matthews picked Sanibel Island as a place to settle, Granny chose the spot with the best shelling. Sanibel Historical Museum and Village notes that soon after arriving, Granny put on the island's first shell show. By 1895, she was hosting guests at the Matthews Hotel, according to the history museum. In ads, the hotel promised newspaper readers a "home-like place" with "excellent cuisine." In 1917, the hotel expanded, and in 1937, it was renamed the Island Inn. In 1955, Granny was remembered as a Sanibel pioneer in her obituary. The family sold the hotel in 1957 to a group who'd been visiting for years. In 2022, much of the property was destroyed by Hurricane Ian, and rebuilding has been taking place since.

If you visit: Stop by the Bailey-Matthews National Shell Museum to see the Great Hall of Shells.

3111 W Gulf Dr.
Sanibel Island, Florida 33957

islandinnsanibel.com

Top: 1910, courtesy of State Library and Archives of Florida
Bottom: Courtesy of Island Inn

COLLIER INN

USEPPA ISLAND

OPENED: 1896 | ROOMS: SEVEN IN THE ORIGINAL HOTEL

WHAT MAKES IT SPECIAL: THOUGH IT'S BEEN DAMAGED BY SEVERAL HURRICANES, THIS HISTORIC HOTEL HAS REINVENTED ITSELF MULTIPLE TIMES.

Like much of Florida, Useppa Island has a long history that includes many people and multiple names, from Giuseppe to Useppi to Useppa to Joseffa, according to the Useppa Island Historical Society. The island's modern history started in 1896 when a streetcar mogul from Chicago bought the island and built a home and hotel. A brief in the *Weekly Tribune* from 1903 described the Useppa Inn as "one of the most delightful resorts along the coast of Florida. On one side rests the placid Charlotte Harbor, while on the other, the surging breakers of the Gulf of Mexico lash the beach for miles, and the tourist, standing upon the hotel verandah, can look out upon countless miles of undulated water in which swim millions of fish awaiting the hook of the angler." An early guest was Barron G. Collier, a New York advertising exec. In 1911, Collier bought the island and the hotel, known as the Tarpon Inn. He added a golf course and built the spot as a haven for tarpon fishing. The hotel expanded, and in the late 1920s, it returned to its original name, Useppa Inn. At one point, the walls of the hotel's restaurant were covered in tarpon scales. Collier died in 1939, and soon the hotel closed because of World War II. In the late 1940s, it suffered damage from a hurricane, and in 1960, the island was used by the CIA to train for a Cuban invasion. Over the next few decades, the island had different owners, got various updates, and suffered more damage from a hurricane. In 1976, it was bought by Garfield Beckstead and for the next 20 years, important discoveries were made about the island's first people, the Calusa. In 1996, the Collier Inn was renovated and reopened as an inn. It took hits from Hurricane Charley in 2004 and Hurricane Ian in 2022. Today, this island, only reachable by boat, is home to Collier Inn, suites, cottages, and its own museum.

IF YOU VISIT: GO TO THE MARINA'S BAR, THE TARPON BAR RESTAURANT, FOR THE HOUSE-MADE CONCH FRITTERS.

USEPPA ISLAND, FLORIDA

useppa.com

Top, middle, bottom right: Courtesy of Collier Inn. *All others:* Circa 1900, courtesy of State Library and Archives of Florida

Belleview Inn

Belleair

Opened: 1897 | Rooms: 35

What makes it special: This Henry Plant hotel is smaller than it once was, but it holds stories of the past with reverence.

Railroad tycoon Henry Plant brought trains to Tampa Bay, and then he built hotels to house his passengers. The first was the Tampa Bay Hotel, and a few years later, he built the Hotel Belleview on Clearwater Harbor. The Queen Anne–style property with 145 original rooms included a golf course and bicycle racing arena, according to Joseph Vars, who worked as the hotel's historian. Henry Plant died in 1899, and his son, Morton Plant, took over the hotel. By 1926, it was known as the Belleview-Biltmore. Like other grand hotels from the era, the hotel was leased to the US military during World War II. It reopened to the public in 1947. Through years of different owners and renovations, 90 percent of the property had been demolished by 2016. In 2018, a smaller version of the hotel opened as the Belleview Inn. Like past guests, visitors to the Belleview will find many diversions, from reading in rocking chairs on the wide veranda and bocce ball to golf and cycling. However, unlike past guests, visitors today will find the Belleview surrounded by modern developments, including homes and condominiums. The building has changed over time, but its history has a safe home in Morton's Reading Room. Artifacts include an early front desk bell, an Edison bulb and socket, and vintage postcards. While tycoons, businessmen, and builders occupy many of the stories behind Florida's great and small hotels, the Belleview has a lady at the center of one of its best stories. Maisie Plant, Morton's wife, gazes out from a portrait in the café named after her. When Morton married Maisie, he traded a mansion on New York City's Fifth Avenue for a string of pearls. The person he traded with? Pierre Cartier. (Cartier still occupies that space.) After Maisie's death, the pearls were sold at auction for a fraction of their value.

IF YOU VISIT: MAKE A TRIP TO THE NEARBY CLEARWATER MARINE AQUARIUM TO MEET THE RESCUED DOLPHINS, SEA TURTLES, AND MANATEES.

25 BELLEVIEW BLVD.
BELLEAIR, FLORIDA 33756

opalcollection.com/belleview-inn

Top Left: Courtesy of Tampa-Hillsborough County Public Library System. *All others:* courtesy of the Belleview Inn

1900s

When the Gilded Age ended, more and more people headed south to Florida for what would become the state's boom years, said historian Joseph Vars. That meant there were more lodgings for regular folks.

"Florida around this time was starting to really cater toward the hoards of average people coming here as well," Vars said.

One of the main draws was the Grapefruit League. Baseball teams from the North came to cities throughout Florida for spring training, said historian Rodney Kite-Powell. And coming with them to watch were more tourists.

"The growth of tourism really dovetails with the growth of a rising middle class in the country," said Lawrence Horwitz, executive vice president of Historic Hotels of America and Historic Hotels Worldwide.

These people weren't the industrialists or the beneficiaries of large trust funds, but they were the professional class, he said, and they had money to spend.

Florida set itself apart during this time for what it offered for the sports vacationers, particularly through fishing, Horwitz noted, which was different than what travelers could find in other places.

The Gibson Inn

Apalachicola

Opened: 1907 | Rooms: 45

What makes it special: This spot has been saved, again and again, by siblings.

The Gibson Inn opened in 1907 as the Franklin Hotel and was viewed as a sign that Apalachicola was on the rise. "One of the big features of any city is a good hotel," the *Pensacola Journal* reported in the fall of 1907. "And in that respect, Apalachicola takes rank with any city on the coast. She has, without doubt, the finest hotel between Jacksonville and Mobile, and one of the finest in the South today." Built by J. F. Buck, "a gentleman of many interests," the hotel had 50 guest rooms, balconies, Turkish rugs, a grand stairway, and electric lights. "Almost any evening will be found the society people of Apalachicola in the Franklin's parlors, chatting or enjoying music, thus making the hotel at once a delightful place to spend a day or so," the article continued. In 1922, sisters Annie Gibson Hayes and Mary Ella Gibson bought the hotel and renamed it the Gibson Inn. The US Army commandeered the hotel during World War II, and by 1977, the hotel was for sale for $75,000. In 1983, it was rescued by the

Koun brothers, who renovated and restored it for a 1985 reopening. In 2018, the Gibson drew another set of siblings, Steven Etchen and Katharine Couillard, who remembered staying at the inn as children. They embarked on further restoration and expansion that will bring another 70 rooms. Visitors today can go shelling and scalloping and can tour Florida's panhandle from the comfort of a golf cart.

IF YOU VISIT: HEAD TO THE HOTEL'S RESTAURANT, THE FRANKLIN CAFÉ, FOR LOCAL OYSTERS SERVED THREE WAYS. IF YOU'RE READY FOR A COCKTAIL, TRY THE CAPTAIN'S GHOST OR GIBSON BREEZE.

51 AVE. C
APALACHICOLA, FLORIDA 32320

gibsoninn.com

Top: Courtesy of Gibson Inn. *Bottom left and middle:* Courtesy of State Library and Archives of Florida. *Bottom right:* Courtesy of Gibson Inn

Selina Miami River

Miami

Opened: 1908 | Rooms: 72

What makes it special: Miami's oldest remaining hotel is a collection of brightly colored former boarding houses nicknamed *The Painted Ladies.*

The nickname refers to the bright colors, and women have been a part of this property from the beginning. According to the nomination form for the National Register of Historic Places, the railroad brought tourists and newcomers to Miami "by the trainload. While the larger, grander hotels such as the Royal Palm attracted such notables as the Rockefellers, Astors, and Vanderbilts, more modest visitors and potential new residents also needed accommodations." And for them, there were rooming houses. In the early 1900s, a group of wooden boarding houses were built along the Miami River alongside the rise of downtown Miami. These properties included Rose Arms, named after Rose Baile, who owned and ran the property with her husband, John. The property became the Miami River Inn and operated as a bed-and-breakfast in the 1990s thanks to the work of preservationist Sally Jude, according to reporting from the *Miami Herald.* In 2015, developer Avra Jain began to work there, adding to her preservation and renovation work of other historic Miami hotels. Today, it's the Selina Miami River, operated by the Latin American company Selina.

If you visit: Order a drink at the hotel's restaurant, Casa Florida, and toast to the women who made sure we can still admire the beautiful architecture.

437 SW 2nd St.
Miami, Florida 33130

selina.com

Top left: 1910, courtesy of State Library and Archives of Florida. *Top right, middle, bottom right:* Courtesy of Selina Miami River. *Bottom left:* Courtesy of Hisory Miami Museum

Chassahowitzka Hotel

Homosassa

Opened: 1910 | Rooms: 4

What makes it special: This old fishing lodge was once the spot to stay for epic hunting and fishing.

In 1910, Ben and Liza Smith bought a large home just steps from the Chassahowitzka River and turned it into a hotel. It passed through three generations of their family, the Stricklands. Early on, reservations for the spot that hunters and fishermen loved were made by mail, according to the *Citrus County Chronicle.* The hotel was sold and subsequently closed in 1969. "The Stricklands always operated the hotel plainly and without pretensions to running a stylish tourist facility," stated an article in the *Tampa Tribune* that year. "For moderate rates they provided comfortable living quarters, set an excellent table and guided sportsmen to the finest fishing and hunting right at the hotel's doorstep." For decades after it closed, the hotel mostly sat empty until it was bought as a private retreat in 1990. In 1991, the road the hotel sits on was named for one of Ben and Liza Smith's daughters, Miss Maggie. She was born in the hotel and was

known as "a longtime fisherwoman, one-time county commissioner and maker of the finest ham sandwich around," the *St. Petersburg Times'* Citrus Edition reported that year. In 2001, a younger member of the Strickland family, David, and his wife, Kimberly, decided it was time for the hotel to reopen, and they bought it back. David died in 2019, and the property is now owned by Seven Sisters Campground.

IF YOU VISIT: STOP BY THREE SISTERS SPRINGS AND TAKE THE BOARDWALK FOR VIEWS OF THE CRYSTAL-CLEAR WATER. WHEN IT'S COLD OUT, MANATEES GATHER THERE TO STAY WARM.

8544 W MISS MAGGIE DR.
HOMOSASSA, FLORIDA 34448

sevensisterscampground.com

Top: Courtesy of Kristen Hare. *Left:* Courtesy of State Library and Archives of Florida
Right: Courtesy of Citrus County Historical Society, Inverness, Florida

The Gasparilla Inn & Club

Boca Grande

Opened: 1911 | Rooms: 137

What makes it special: This posh spot often hosted a slew of powerful American businessmen.

In 1909, the Boca Grande Land Company built a resort on Gasparilla Island that opened for the season in 1911. A newspaper ad called the spot the "most prolific tarpon fishing grounds known" and "absolutely the most modern and up-to-date hotel in South Florida." A year later, the hotel expanded and was renamed the Gasparilla Inn. According to the hotel, early guests included the tycoons of the time, from Henry Plant and Henry Ford to J. P. Morgan. Barron Collier, the New York ad exec who purchased nearby Useppa Island, bought the inn in 1930 and added guest cottages to the property. For years, guests arrived by train until the Boca Grande Causeway was finished in 1958. In the 1960s, Bayard Sharp bought the inn and set about expanding and restoring it for the rest of his life, through 2002. That included trading some of the

Left: 1915, Courtesy of State Library and Archives of Florida
Right: 1920, Courtesy of State Library and Archives of Florida

inn's oceanfront property in the 1980s for an abandoned railroad right of way, now used by guests as a bike path. Sharp's daughter Sarah and her husband, William Farrish, now own the Gasparilla Inn.

IF YOU VISIT: YOU DON'T HAVE TO BE A GUEST TO STOP BY ITS RESTAURANT, THE PINK ELEPHANT, WHICH SHARP RENOVATED AND REOPENED IN 1980. TRY THE HUMMER, THE SIGNATURE COCKTAIL MADE WITH VANILLA ICE CREAM, MT. GAY RUM, AND KAHLUA.

500 PALM AVE.
BOCA GRANDE, FLORIDA 33921

the-gasparilla-inn.com

Top: Photos by Carmel Brantley. *Bottom left:* Courtesy of Hampton Dunn Collection of Florida Postcards. *Bottom right:* Courtesy of Digital Commonwealth

Old Colorado Inn

Stuart

Opened: 1914 | Rooms: 24

What makes it special: Two historic hotels make up this property in a pedestrian-friendly downtown that looks out on the St. Lucie River.

The Old Colorado Inn, Stuart is more than just one historic hotel. It's two historic hotels plus six historic homes and cottages. The first, Coventry Hotel, opened in 1914 and made news because it offered electricity in every room nearly a decade before homes around the country made the switch from gas. The Coventry eventually was converted into apartments until it was purchased in 2012 and became part of the Old Colorado Inn. The second hotel that's now part of the property was the Clifton Guest and Fishing Lodge, also built in 1914. In 2018, when it was slated to be torn down and turned into condominiums, Old Colorado Inn owners Steven and Ashley Vitale made the case for preserving it and adding to the inn's lodgings. Among the Old Colorado Inn's six historic homes and cottages is the iconic Owl House. Built in 1904, this home has a four-pointed gabled

roof meant to withstand strong winds that gives the building the look of an owl's head. The Ernest Lyons House is also part of the inn's properties. This 1890 home is a designated Florida Literary Landmark thanks to author and journalist Ernest Lyons, who lived in the home from 1937 to 1990.

IF YOU VISIT: STROLL THROUGH DOWNTOWN STUART, WHERE YOU'LL FIND SHOPPING, RESTAURANTS, AND A COURTESY TRAM TO GET YOU AROUND.

211 S COLORADO AVE.
STUART, FLORIDA 34994

oldcoloradoinn.com

Top, bottom left, middle: Courtesy of the Old Colorado Inn
Bottom right: Courtesy of Sandra Thurlow

CRYSTAL BAY HOTEL

ST. PETERSBURG

OPENED: 1916 | ROOMS: 60

WHAT MAKES IT SPECIAL: FROM THE HOTEL'S VERANDA, GUESTS HAVE A PERFECT VIEW OF THE SUNSET.

Crystal Bay Hotel opened as Sunset Apartment Hotel in 1916. With views looking out onto Boca Ciega Bay, the property offered kitchenettes and a third-floor sun parlor. The hotel remained open during the ups and downs in the decades that followed, including wars, the Great Depression, and a tourism boom. Guests are rumored to have included Babe Ruth, Marilyn Monroe, and F. Scott and Zelda Fitzgerald. In 1958, the hotel was remodeled and turned into a year-round property. By the 1980s, the hotel had become a retirement home. In 2007, it reopened as the Parkview Hotel but struggled to return to its more glamorous days. A few years later, the building sat empty and was used for training by local SWAT teams. In 2015, the hotel was renovated and reopened as Crystal Bay Hotel. The views that first drew builders to the spot are still postcard-perfect.

IF YOU VISIT: ST. PETERSBURG HAS A HANDFUL OF HISTORIC HOTELS, INCLUDING WHAT'S NOW THE DOWNTOWN COURTYARD BY MARRIOTT, THE AVALON, HOLLANDER HOTEL, AND THE BIRCHWOOD. VISIT THE BIRCHWOOD'S ROOFTOP BAR, THE CANOPY, FOR STUNNING WATER VIEWS.

7401 CENTRAL AVE.
ST. PETERSBURG, FLORIDA 33710

crystalbayhotel.com

1920s

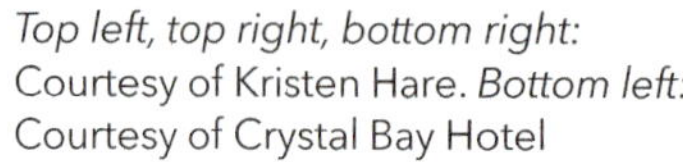

Top left, top right, bottom right: Courtesy of Kristen Hare. *Bottom left:* Courtesy of Crystal Bay Hotel

By the 1920s, Florida's population was doubling every few years, said historian Joseph Vars. And the sunshine state was starting to define its aesthetic—a Mediterranean style with various other flavors sprinkled in. It added to the state's exotic feel, Vars said.

"I call this the era of Florida's great Spanish hotels," he said.

Post-World War I, there was more money, said Historic Hotels of America's Lawrence Horwitz.

"And with more money came resources. The architects were being asked to design something more stately, more magical, more unique and more memorable," he said. "You have the evolution of an architectural style that is partially taken from architecture in Europe but then produced on a much grander level."

Hotels during this era were often built around grand gardens, with courtyards and public spaces. The rooms were more modern than their earlier counterparts, with electricity, ceiling fans, private bathrooms and even bathtubs.

The boom continued until it collapsed with the real estate market in the middle of the 1920s. Vars thinks it was a harbinger of the coming Great Depression. Florida was, he said, a "bubble in the sun."

Top left, top right: Courtesy of Hilton
Bottom: Courtesy of State Library and Archives of Florida

Casa Marina

Key West

Opened: 1920 | Rooms: 311

What makes it special: Though more than 100 years old, Casa Marina was the most modern of the Florida East Coast Railway hotels.

"The latest chain of famous hotels operated by the Florida East Coast Hotel Company was opened here today for the reception of guests," the *Lakeland Evening Telegram* reported on January 1, 1921. "It is called La Casa Marina, which means 'the house by the sea,' and the appropriateness of its title is evident to all visitors." Dreamt up by Henry Flagler, who died nearly a decade before it opened, the hotel was the newest destination for his Florida East Coast Railway. The property was designed by Thomas Hastings and John M. Carrere, the architects behind the Metropolitan Opera House and the Public Library in New York City and the Senate and House of Representative buildings in Washington, DC. In 1942, it was acquired by the US Navy. After the war, the building returned to being a hotel but was commandeered again in 1962 during the Cuban Missile Crisis. In 1966, the hotel was the training ground for US Peace Corps volunteers. It sat mostly empty until 1976 when it was purchased and renovated. Since then, it's had multiple owners and makeovers. In 2022, it became part of Hilton's Curio Collection, and in 2023, it was renovated yet again. Today, Casa Marina has Key West's largest private beach and the brightly decorated Canary Room, named after Ernest Hemingway's "A Canary for One."

If you visit: Sunsets are a big deal in many parts of Florida. At Key West's Mallory Square, there's an entire nightly festival for it.

**1500 Reynolds St.
Key West, Florida 33040**

casamarinaresort.com

Hotel Cordova, St. Petersburg, Florida.
HOTEL CORDOVA
CORDOVA INN
HOTEL CORDOVA

The Cordova Inn

St. Petersburg

Opened: 1921 | Rooms: 32

What makes it special: While palatial hotels were popular in this era, this hotel is an example of what was available for everyday tourists.

The Cordova Inn opened as Hotel Scott in 1921 in downtown St. Petersburg. The small, neoclassical hotel was open for Florida winters in its early years and offered visitors more modest and lower-priced accommodations than some of the area's swankier options. It went through various ownership over the years, and by 1926, it was called Hotel Cordova. In 2000, the hotel was renamed the Pier Hotel for its proximity to St. Petersburg's pier. During these years, the hotel was pink. By 2015, the hotel had sold again and reopened as the Cordova Inn. Most recently, it became part of the New Hotel Collection.

If you visit: Head over to St. Pete's Pier where you'll find art installations, a playground, and spots to fish, dine, and watch for dolphins. There's also a speedy and free trolley that offers rides from end to end.

253 2nd Ave. N
St. Petersburg, Florida 33701

cordovainnstpete.com

Top left: Courtesy of the Cordova Inn. *Bottom left:* Courtesy of Tampa-Hillsborough County Public Library System. *Right column:* Courtesy of Kristen Hare

Hamilton Hotel

Winter Park, Florida

Dining Room

OPENS

Wednesday, Feb. 3rd.

Breakfast
7 to 9

Lunch
12:30 to 2

Dinner
6 to 8

Bridge Luncheons
Bridge luncheon upon request

Under new management, the Hamilton hotel dining room opens Wednesday morning to resume its place among the first class dining rooms in Winter Park.

Fully realizing the popularity of this dining room in the past, the present management awaits your approval of their efforts toward the proper atmosphere, good food correctly and properly served.

Hamilton Hotel

DINING ROOM

Winter Park, Florida

Park Plaza Hotel

Winter Park

Opened: 1922 | Rooms: 28

What makes it special: The second-floor balconies looking out onto Park Avenue and Central Park are a fantastic spot for morning coffee or an evening libation.

The Park Plaza Hotel opened in 1922 as the Hamilton Hotel. Over the decades, the hotel hosted baseball players in spring training, guests from up north, and countless community events. For 26 years, Mr. and Mrs. Millard Rotter operated the Hamilton as a winter destination. In 1976, they retired and the hotel opened for the first time as a year-round location, according to press reports from the time. One year later, it was purchased by John and Cissie Spang, and it became thc Park Plaza. The Spangs' daughters, Suzy and Mindy, run the hotel today. It has several original features, including the huge fireplace in the lobby and the original Jacksonville Elevator Company elevator. Both are still in use.

If you visit: Stroll down Park Avenue, where you'll find boutiques, restaurants, and bars to explore.

307 S Park Ave.
Winter Park, Florida 32789

parkplazahotel.com

Top left: 1926, *Orlando Sentinel*. *Top and middle right:* Courtesy of Park Plaza Hotel
Bottom left: Courtesy of Kristen Hare. *Bottom right:* Courtesy of State Library and Archives of Florida

Top: 1900, courtesy of State Library and Archives of Florida. *Bottom right:* Courtesy of State Library and Archives of Florida. *Middle:* State Library and Archives of Florida *Bottom left:* Courtesy of Kristen Hare

Terrace Hotel

Lakeland

Opened: 1924 | Rooms: 88

What makes it special: While Lakeland has changed in the last century, the stunning views of Lake Mirror from the hotel have not.

Before Hotel Lakeland Terrace opened in 1924, the Tremont Hotel, opened in the late 1800s, stood in its place, according to newspaper records. It came down so the Terrace could go up. The Hotel Lakeland Terrace had sisters in Tampa and Sarasota, and the 10-story spot overlooking Lake Mirror promised that it was "fireproof throughout and modern in every respect" in a 1924 ad. Unlike many Florida hotels at the time, the Terrace was open all year and offered air-conditioning. But like many other Florida hotels, it struggled in the 1970s. In 1986, the hotel was the home of 42 residents, many elderly, when it was closed due to a fire hazard, the press reported. In the 1990s, Lakeland residents were working on renovating downtown and the hotel along with it. In 1995, the city of Lakeland bought a piece of land next door to help ensure its preservation, and three years later, the hotel reopened. It's been through multiple owners and renovations since and currently is part of Hilton's Tapestry Collection. Like it was when it first opened, the Terrace is once again "modern in every respect."

If you visit: See another piece of history while you're in Lakeland and visit the only college campus designed by renowned architect Frank Lloyd Wright. Florida Southern, known as the Child of the Sun, offers guided and self-guided tours.

329 E Main St.
Lakeland, Florida 33801

hilton.com

Top left: 1923, *St. Petersburg Times*, *Top right:* Courtesy of Tampa-Hillsborough County Public Library System, *All others:* Courtesy of Marriott International

Vinoy

St. Petersburg

Opened: 1925 | Rooms: 346

What makes it special: St. Petersburg's pink hotel includes glimpses of its past throughout, making it easy to connect with its stories and history.

St. Petersburg's most iconic hotel started off as a lark. In 1923, after a night of food and drinks at the home of businessman Aymer Vinoy Laughner, a professional golfer was showing off his skills. Another guest, a real estate developer, noted that where his balls were landing would be a perfect waterfront property. "Build a hotel over there . . . and call it Vinoy, since that's such a pretty name," wrote grandson Niles Laughner in a book on the hotel's history. Construction for the Vinoy began in 1925 and the hotel opened that year on New Year's Eve. According to Laughner, the paint was still wet that night, but the staff were ready to put on a show. That activity would continue until 1942, when the hotel was leased to the United States military for housing during World War II, according to the hotel. It emerged afterward as a popular spot with travelers, but by the 1970s, it fell so low that rooms cost just $7 a night, according to Historic Hotels of America. The Vinoy closed in 1974, and stories from those days include rogue volleyball games in the once-grand ballroom and alligators on the lower level after flooding. In 1978, St. Petersburg citizens rallied to protect the property, and in 1992, it reopened. The Vinoy has had several owners since, most recently Marriott International making it part of its Autograph Collection.

If you visit: Stop by the hotel's bars, restaurants, and shops for a visit, or go deeper with the delightful history tour and tea.

501 5th Ave. NE
St. Petersburg, Florida 33701

thevinoy.com

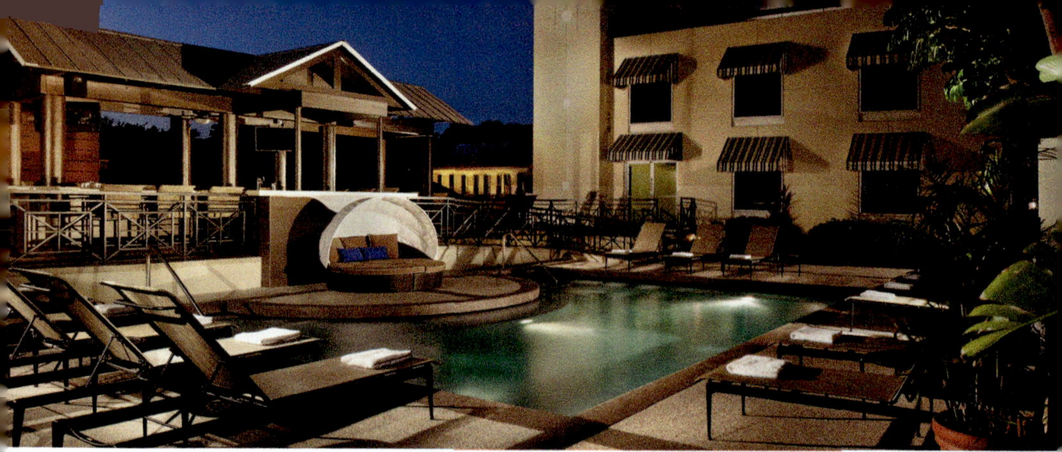

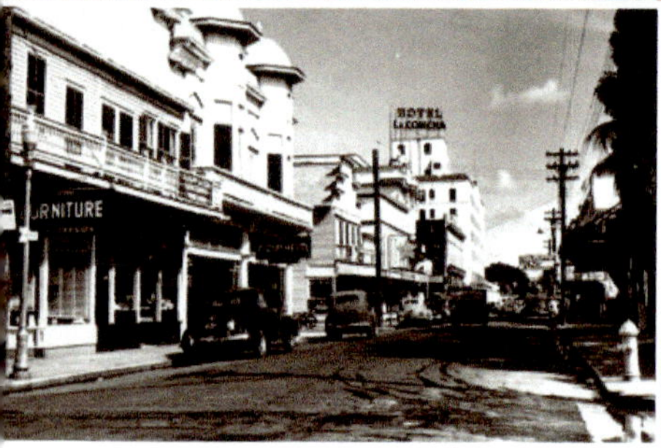
HOTEL
LACONCHA

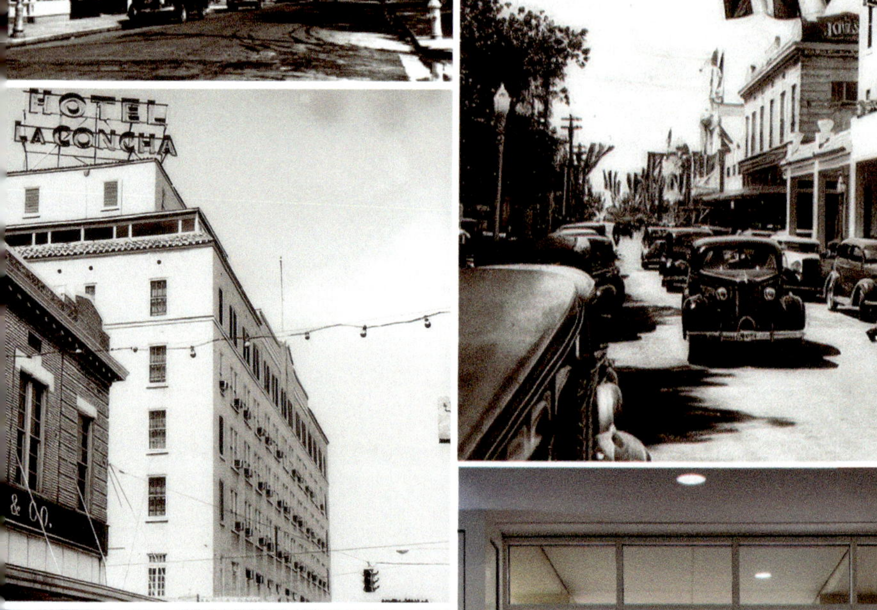

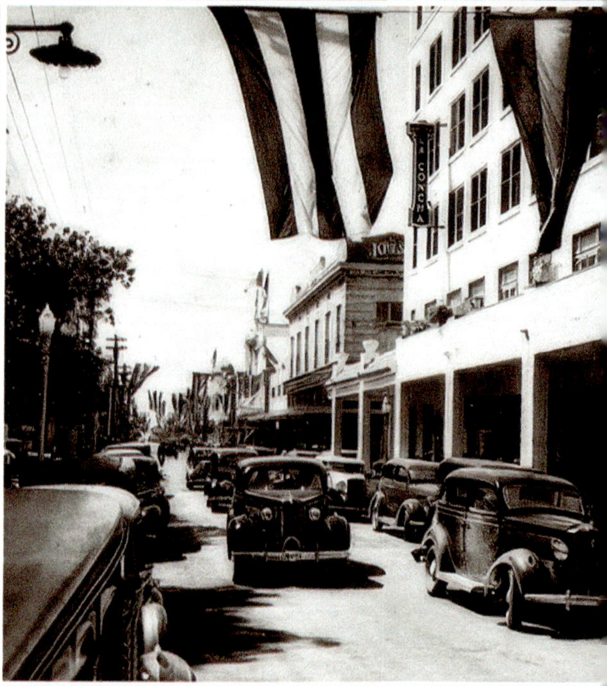
LA CONCHA

HOTEL
LACONCHA

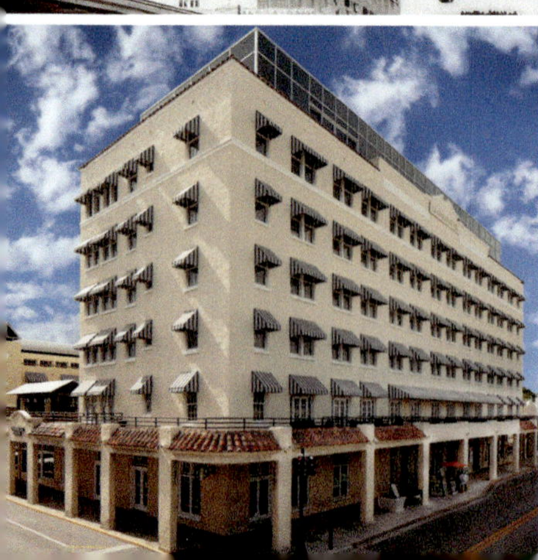

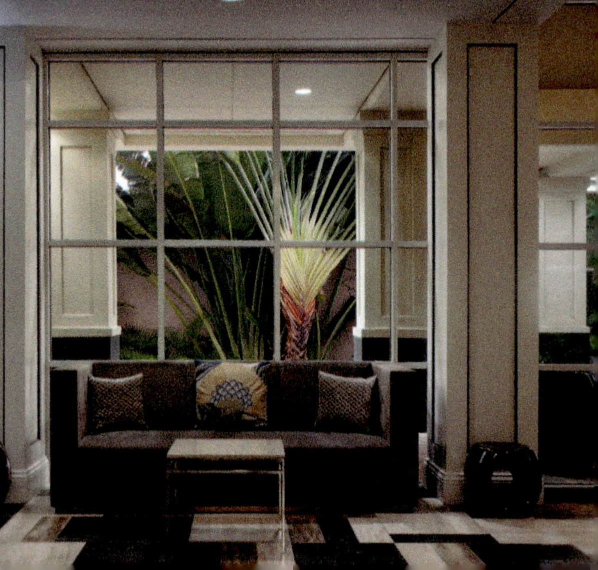

La Concha

Key West

Opened: 1926 | Rooms: 171

What makes it special: This six-story hotel was home to Tennessee Williams while he wrote a masterpiece.

La Concha opened in Key West in 1926, earning its name from a contest. The winning name wasn't popular with the locals, the *Palm Beach Post* reported in 1927. "Key Westers of a better class dislike the term 'conch.' Therefore it can readily be understood that La Concha as a name for one of the finest hotels is equivalent to flirting a red blanket in the face of a bull." The hotel was built by Carl Aubuchon as Key West's tourism industry started booming. With the Great Depression and a hurricane in 1935, it wouldn't last. But a few great American writers rediscovered it. The *Miami Herald* reported the hotel was where playwright Tennessee Williams wrote *A Streetcar Named Desire,* and the hotel is featured in Ernest Hemingway's *To Have and Have Not.* The hotel has had different makeovers and owners over the years. Today it's a Marriott hotel and a modern space in a fascinating old city.

If you visit: Tour Ernest Hemingway's home and museum and meet the descendants of Snow White, Hemingway's six-toed cat.

430 Duval St.
Key West, Florida 33040

marriott.com

Courtesy of Marriott International

SWIMMING POOL AT MIAMI-BILTMORE HOTEL, MIAMI, FLORIDA

THE BILTMORE

CORAL GABLES

OPENED: 1926 | ROOMS: 271

WHAT MAKES IT SPECIAL: THE 23,000-SQUARE-FOOT POOL HERE HAS DELIGHTED VISITORS FOR NEARLY 100 YEARS.

Like the city itself that sits just outside Miami, the Biltmore was built by George Merrick and John McEntee Bowman. Then known as the Miami-Biltmore Hotel, it opened in 1926 and soon became the spot to be seen. The merriment ended abruptly in 1942 when the Biltmore became a military hospital. It stayed open until 1968 as a Veterans Administration hospital. For decades, like its once-grand sister hotels around the state, the hotel sat empty. Coral Gables got ownership in 1973, began renovations a decade later, and the hotel reopened in 1987. By 1990, it closed again. The inn "outlived hurricanes and weathered neglect," a *Miami Herald* article read, but it "succumbed Tuesday under the crush of debt." Two years later, Seaway Hotels Group bought the hotel and golf course and started a 10-year renovation. The hotel's famous pool, thought to be one of the largest in the United States, is 23,000 square feet and just as magnificent now as it was nearly 100 years ago.

IF YOU VISIT: SPEAKING OF SWIMMING, PACK YOUR SWIMSUIT AND STOP BY THE REMARKABLE VENETIAN POOL, A SPRING-FED BEAUTY WITH WATERFALLS AND GROTTOS THAT FIRST OPENED IN 1923.

1200 ANASTASIA AVE.
CORAL GABLES, FLORIDA 33134

biltmorehotel.com

Top row, middle left, and bottom right: Courtesy of The Biltmore. *Middle right and bottom left:* 1900, 1925 courtesy of State Library and Archives of Florida, respectively

Top: Courtesy of Fred Mays. *Middle*: Courtesy of Maxwell MacKenzie *Bottom*: Courtesy of Tarpon Lodge

Tarpon Lodge

Bookelia

Opened: 1926 | Rooms: 20, plus two cottages

What makes it special: The sunset views at Tarpon Lodge are one of a kind.

Tarpon Lodge has had a lot of names but one big draw. It started as a fishing shack built by Graham and Mary Wilson in 1926. The Pennsylvania couple named their winter escape Gra-Mar Villa and built his-and-hers boathouses. In 1945, the property became an upscale fishing spot, renamed Pine-Aire Lodge. From 1955 through 1980, it was known as Pala Mar and used as a retreat and training site for the American Bible College. In 1980, it was used as a drug and alcohol rehabilitation facility, and a second building, the Island House, was added. The Wells family bought the property in 1999 and began restoring it as Tarpon Lodge and Restaurant, which opened the following year. The family also runs nearby Cabbage Key Inn. In 2004, the spot took a hit from Hurricane Charley, and the two boathouses were knocked off their foundations. The roof and walls survived, and they were rebuilt as the Boathouse, a one-bedroom cottage. The Tarpon Lodge's restaurant offers incredible food and views from the original charming 1926 home.

If you visit: On the way to or from the lodge, stop in tiny Matlacha (pronounced Mat-la-shay) and shop the funky boutiques and galleries.

13771 Waterfront Dr.
Bookelia, Florida 33922

tarponlodge.com

The Jacaranda

AT AVON PARK

Welcomes You To Florida

We urge you to come and enjoy our wonderful climate and beautiful auton drives, at the same time seeing some of the outstanding attractions of the state whi located in this section of Florida. We especially call your attention to The Mou Lake Sanctuary and Singing Tower, Highlands Hammock—a natural tropical g and the thousands of acres of bearing citrus groves. Hundreds of fresh water lakes invi visitor to come and catch his share of the big-mouth black bass with which they are

The Jacaranda Hotel Offers

FREE BOAT RIDES AND FISHING TRIPS FOR OUR GUESTS

STEAM HEAT	ROOM PHONES	ELEVATOR SERVICE
SPACIOUS LOBBY	PALM ROOM	VERANDAS
ALL OUTSIDE ROOMS	MODERN CONVENIENCES	REASONABLE PRICES

DINING ROOM AND COFFEE SHOPPE (EXCELLENT FOOD AND SERVICE)

RATES (*European Plan*)

Single, $1.50 to $3.00 per day.
Double, $2.50 to $6.00 per day.
Parties of four or more $1.00 each.
Special weekly or monthly rates.
Reasonable American Plan Rates.

Be Sure and See Highlands Hamm

2000 ACRES OF NATURAL TROPICAL GARD

Bottom: Courtesy of *Tampa Bay Times*. *Middle right:* Courtesy of State Library and Archives of Florida. *All other photos:* Courtesy of Hotel Jacaranda

The Hotel Jacaranda

Avon Park

Opened: 1926 | Rooms: 31

What makes it special: The hotel and the restaurant inside have operated since they first opened.

The Hotel Jacaranda might be the only establishment in this book named after the thing it replaced. Construction on Main Street in Avon Park began in 1923 when a 150-year-old jacaranda tree was cut down to make room for the hotel. Built by John Raab and Harry Winters in the Spanish style, the hotel opened in 1926 and was a steady home to baseball players, including the St. Louis Cardinals, who stayed here from 1927 to 1929 during spring training. The property came to be known as the Jac or "Queen of the Ridge." "Avon Park is near the center of 90 percent of the population of the state," the *Miami Herald* reported in 1934, "with fine roads leading in and out. Tourists are finding that they can make the city their headquarters and see most of Florida slowly and pleasantly on short trips." In the 1940s, the hotel was the home to young pilots in training for World War II. During recent renovations, a love letter to one of them from a forlorn young woman was found tucked behind one of the hotel room's mirrors. The Jac had several owners over the years and was bought by the South Florida State College Foundation in 1988. Visitors can still stop by the hotel's restaurant for lunch and dinner. If you visit, you might hear the music of pianist Jeff Klein, who's been playing in the Jac's lobby for 30 years.

If you visit: Head nearby to Maxwell Groves Country Store for the best homemade orange ice cream.

19 E Main St.
Avon Park, Florida 33825

hoteljac.com

Top: Circa 1900, courtesy of State Library and Archives of Florida. *Middle:* 1981, courtesy of State Library and Archives of Florida. *Bottom Row:* Courtesy of Kristen Hare

HOTEL CASSADAGA

CASSADAGA

OPENED: 1927 | ROOMS: 12

WHAT MAKES IT SPECIAL: THE GHOSTS ARE QUITE WELCOME HERE.

The Cassadaga Hotel opened in the 1920s as more and more people visited the community where a spiritualist camp and community were forming, according to the Orange County Regional History Center. In 1933, the camp association sold the hotel, "advertising a kind of general supernatural appeal to its visitors," the history center reported. In the late 1940s, Margaret McGill became the hotel's owner and she opened it year-round starting in 1955. In 1962, the hotel was sold to the Spiritualists Benelovent Society Inc., according to a brief in *the Orlando Sentinel.* Regardless of ownership, the hotel has long been a spot for hospitality to the living and the dead. In 2007, a *Tampa Tribune* photographer visited and wrote about the images he took in the hotel's lobby. "I can honestly say that in my six years shooting photographs for this newspaper, I've never seen anything quite like what we got on film. It looks like this weird little glowing ball in one corner, and in the other corner a reflection, in glass, of what looks eerily like a child's face. When I told our innkeeper about it, he was decidedly unimpressed. 'Oh yeah,' he said. 'Our guests get photos like this all the time. I have no idea what it is. I just know it's there.'" Today, visitors to the hotel can book all sorts of experiences, including psychic readings, healing sessions and past-life regressions. Who knows, maybe you've been to the Cassadaga before . . .

IF YOU VISIT: SEE A MEDIUM, OF COURSE.

355 CASSADAGA RD.
CASSADAGA, FLORIDA 32744

hotelcassadaga.com

Top and bottom: Courtesy of the Fenway. *Middle:* Courtesy of Tampa-Hillsborough County Public Library System

FENWAY HOTEL

DUNEDIN

OPENED: 1927 | ROOMS: 83

WHAT MAKES IT SPECIAL: THE FENWAY HAS LIVED MANY LIVES, FROM SWANKY HOTEL TO RADIO STATION TO PRIVATE SCHOOL. IT'S ONCE AGAIN A HOTEL, AND IT'S ONE WITH A LOT OF SOUL.

Dunedin's Fenway calls itself "a place humming with soul." That's pretty accurate, and not just because its latest incarnation has a musical theme. Construction on the hotel began in 1924, and even before the hotel officially opened, it was a place of music. From 1925 to 1927, the Fenway's rooftop housed Pinellas County's first radio station, WGHB. When the hotel opened in early January of 1927, a four-piece orchestra played for guests and visitors, according to news reports from the time. It thrived as a winter hotel but faltered as the hotel and tourist industry modernized. In 1961, the Fenway closed and became the campus of Trinity Bible College. In 1991, it became the campus of Schiller International University. By the 2000s, the "Grand Lady of Dunedin" was covered in graffiti and sat vacant as plans for renovation, expansion, and revival faltered. In 2014, the Taoist Tai Chi Society of the United States of America presented a plan to renovate the property. The Fenway reopened in 2018 with a preserved speakeasy, a stage in the lobby, and a hotel playlist. Now, it's part of Marriott's Autograph Collection.

IF YOU VISIT: WHILE YOU CAN'T GO INTO THE OLD SPEAKEASY ANYMORE, HEAD TO HI-FI ROOFTOP BAR FOR STUNNING VIEWS OF ST. JOSEPH'S SOUND AND CLEVERLY CONCOCTED DRINKS, LIKE THE ABSINTHE-MINDED TOURIST.

453 EDGEWATER DR.
DUNEDIN, FLORIDA 34698

fenwayhotel.com

Top and bottom: Courtesy of Kristen Hare. *Middle left:* Courtesy of Hampton Dunn Collection of Florida Postcards. *Middle right:* Courtesy of the Hacienda

The Hacienda

New Port Richey

Opened: 1927 | Rooms: 40

What makes it special: The Hacienda is one of Florida's beloved and revived pink hotels.

Because of the Hacienda hotel, New Port Richey became known as "Hollywood East" in the late 1920s, the *Tampa Bay Times* reported. The Spanish Colonial Revival–style hotel opened in 1927 and soon became the hot spot for the stars, including Gloria Swanson and Charlie Chaplin. "It is easy for one who gets his first view of the Hacienda Hotel to wonder if he is in dreamland," the *Tampa Tribune* reported that year. The furnishings and the land were donated by James Meighan, brother of silent film actor Thomas Meighan, and he, his wife, and their friends became the hotel's first guests. The hotel includes a half floor where booze was thought to be smuggled in during Prohibition. The Hacienda continued operating over the decades that followed but suffered the same realities as many of its era. By the 1980s, it was a home for people with special needs, the *Times* reported. The city bought it in 2003 and closed it three years later. Jim Gunderson, owner of Lakeside Inn in Mount Dora, started renovations in 2019, and the hotel opened again in 2022. "In Florida, many beauties are unveiled to those from the frozen north who come to visit us," a *Tribune* reporter wrote in 1927. "But it is said nowhere in the state is there a more delightful, a more satisfying picture of a part of 'old Spain' set down in such a natural beauty spot as the Hacienda Hotel, a name that is truly indicative of what it signifies."

If you visit: Attend an event at the Richey Suncoast Theatre, which opened as the Meighan Theatre in 1926.

5621 Main St.
New Port Richey, Florida 34652

haciendahotelnpr.com

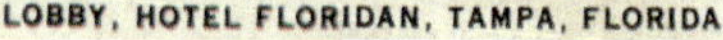

Top left: Courtesy of Kristen Hare. *Middle left:* Courtesy of Hampton Dunn Collection of Florida Postcards. *Middle right:* Courtesy of State Library and Archives of Florida. *Top right and bottom:* Courtesy of Hotel Flor

HOTEL FLOR

TAMPA

OPENED: 1927 | ROOMS: 212

WHAT MAKES IT SPECIAL: THE HOTEL FLORIDAN SIGN ON THE HOTEL FLOR'S ROOFTOP IS AN ICONIC PART OF TAMPA'S SKYLINE.

Stretching 19 stories high, the Hotel Floridan was built by a Canadian developer and opened in 1927. "The building has the distinction of being the tallest as well as one of the largest hotels in Florida," read a newspaper announcement from that year. Unlike the winter getaways springing up around the state, the Floridan had a different purpose. "It has 400 rooms and 400 baths. The hotel is now open for business and caters to commercial men." The Floridan was a vibrant spot for decades, hosting travelers, business leaders, and soldiers. The hotel's popular Sapphire Room was rumored to be a great place to find love, at least temporarily. By the 1980s, the earlier glamour had faded, and the hotel closed in 1987. The Floridan faced a demolition order in 2005, but it was renovated and reopened as the Floridan Palace in 2012. That year, it again became a place for the powerful when it hosted the Republican National Convention. The hotel was renovated and renamed Hotel Flor in 2023 as part of Hilton's Tapestry Collection. The famed Sapphire Room is now the Dan, and there's still a lot to love about its speakeasy-inspired vibes.

IF YOU VISIT: HEAD DOWN SOUTH FLORIDA AVENUE AND STOP BY AN OLD BUILDING THAT'S NOW A NEW HOTEL, THE LE MERIDIEN TAMPA. THIS SPOT'S FIRST LIFE WAS AS A FEDERAL COURTHOUSE, AND THE GRANDEUR REMAINS. TRY THE BAR, RESTAURANT, OR COFFEE SHOP TO SEE MORE.

905 N FLORIDA AVE.
TAMPA, FLORIDA 33602

hotelflortampa.com

EDGEWATER HOTEL
Park Entrance to Pier on Lake Apopka, Winter Garden, Florida
EDGEWATER
HOTEL
The Chef's Table
Edgewater
99 W. PLANT ST

EDGEWATER HOTEL

WINTER GARDEN

OPENED: 1927 | ROOMS: 15

WHAT MAKES IT SPECIAL: NOW A BED-AND-BREAKFAST, THIS HOTEL IS PART OF A STILL-THRIVING DOWNTOWN.

The three-story brick Edgewater Hotel opened on New Year's Day of 1927 with a housewarming party that included dinner and dancing until midnight, according to news reports from the time. After opening, the *Orlando Sentinel* regularly published the names and hometowns of the hotel's guests. A newspaper ad for the hotel from 1927 read, "Our motto: the sweetest thing on earth is the pleasure of pleasing." Thanks to its proximity to Lake Apopka, the hotel added a fish-cleaning station on each floor in the 1930s. Pollution in the area affected the number of visitors to Lake Apopka, and eventually, the hotel business in Winter Garden suffered, too. In the 1940s, the US Army housed soldiers at Edgewater as they prepared to deploy for World War II. By the 1950s, the hotel closed and was turned into apartments. Workers reportedly stayed there while building nearby Walt Disney World in Orlando. The building closed completely in 1968 and was considered a blight in Winter Garden for decades. After eight years of restoration, it got a new life and reopened as a bed-and-breakfast in 2003.

IF YOU VISIT: MANY CENTRAL FLORIDA TOWNS ARE PACKED WITH CHARM, INCLUDING DOWNTOWN WINTER GARDEN. CHECK OUT THE SHOPS, RESTAURANTS, AND GREAT PEOPLE-WATCHING ALONG PLANT STREET.

99 W PLANT ST.
WINTER GARDEN, FLORIDA 34787

historicedgewater.com

Top and bottom: Courtesy of Kristen Hare. *Middle left:* Courtesy of Digital Commonwealth. *Middle right:* Courtesy of Winter Garden Historical Society

PUTNAM
LODGE

Putnam Hotel

Shamrock

Opened: 1927 | Rooms: 26

What makes it special: The interior is covered in pecky cypress that was hand-stenciled when the lodge first opened.

Thirty-one years after it opened, the Putnam Lodge was up for sale along with the town in which it was located in the Florida panhandle. "That's right, there's a complete town for sale," the *Tampa Tribune* reported in 1958. Both the lodge and the town, Shamrock, were established in the 1920s with the rise of the lumber industry. A large part of its business was housing executives of Putnam Lumber Company. It sat vacant for almost seven years before Beverly and Ed Pivacek purchased it in 2013. Beverly had tried to buy the lodge back in the 1970s when her parents moved to the area, but it was sold to another buyer. The inside is covered with pecky cypress decorated with hand-stenciling. Visitors today will find peacocks, chickens, and guinea fowl roaming the large grounds. There's also a 60-space RV park and the 1927 Steak House restaurant. Al Capone was a well-known guest, and there's a room named after him, as well as a hidden room and getaway staircase that locals, including one barber, report was used by the notorious gangster.

If you visit: Eat at 1927 Steak House and try the Putnam fried brussels sprouts and Bev's bread pudding.

15487 NW Hwy. 19
Cross City, Florida 32628

putnamlodge.com

Top and bottom left: Courtesy of Kristen Hare. *Top right:* Courtesy of Hampton Dunn Collection of Florida Postcards. *Middle right:* Courtesy of State Library and Archives of Florida. *Bottom right:* Courtesy of Joseph Vars

Bottom right: Courtesy of Tampa-Hillsborough County Public Library System. *All other photos:* Courtesy of The Don CeSar

The Don CeSar

St. Pete Beach

Opened: 1928 | Rooms: 277

What makes it special: It's known as "The Pink Palace" and is a landmark on the beach.

"You may revel in relaxation and repose, or employ yourself with any and all of the manifold activities—bathing, boating, fishing, golfing, dancing, playing cards, or the indoor and outdoor shuffleboards—enjoying gorgeous sunrises and sublime sunsets," read a newspaper ad from 1928. "Many attractions invite you to come and tarry at the Don CeSar—hotel without pattern, precedent or parallel, and the 'Glory of the Gulf.'" The Don CeSar opened in January of 1928 and was called the "largest, finest hotel on the Gulf of Mexico" by the *St. Petersburg Times*. In 1942, the US Army bought the hotel to house injured service members returning from World War II. Three years later, it became a Veterans Administration headquarters. By 1969, the Pink Palace, as it was known, was in trouble from decades of neglect and disuse. A 1970 newspaper story called it the "pink elephant," "inhabited only by rats and a custodian." Another article that same year deemed it "an unwanted ghost owned by the US Government." Thanks to a "Save the Don" campaign, the once-grand hotel got a second chance when it was purchased and renovated by William Bowman. The hotel has been through multiple renovations and owners since, adding shops, a spa, and several restaurants. Today it is owned by Host Hotels and Resorts and is once again an icon on the beach.

If you visit: Consider getting a day pass to relax by the pool. The restaurants, spa, and shopping at the Don are equally worth exploring and enjoying.

3400 Gulf Blvd.
St. Pete Beach, Florida 33706

doncesar.com

MONROE TOWERS
Eskay
DRUGS

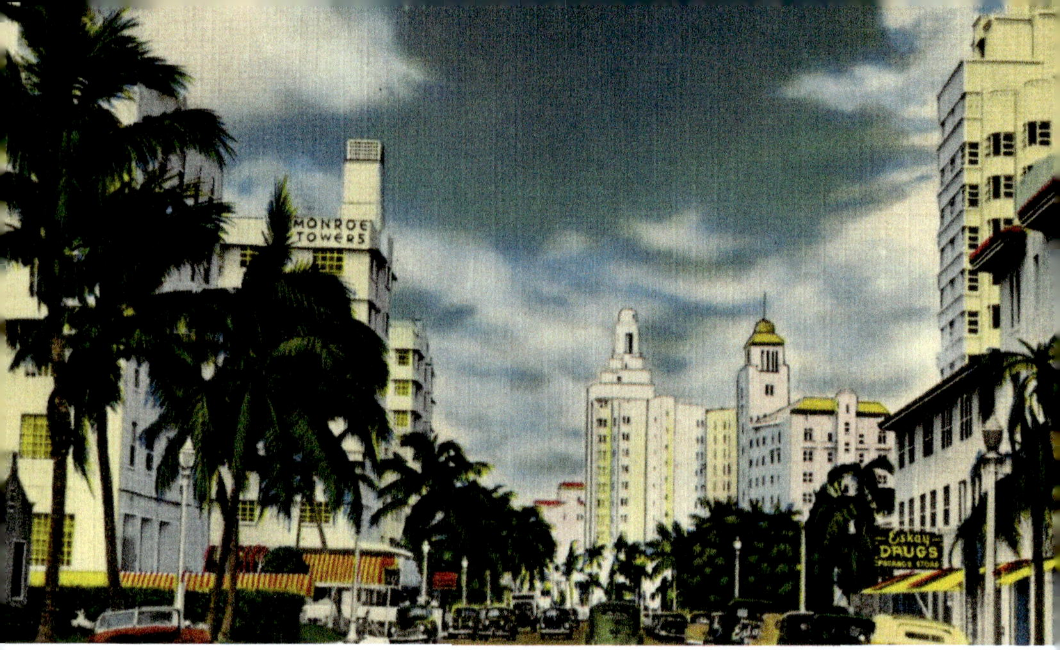

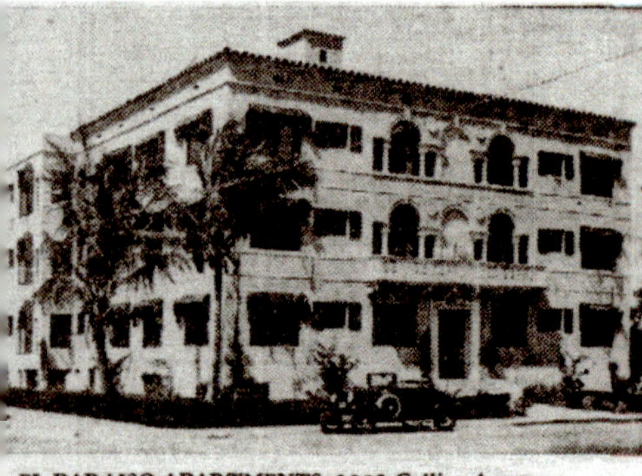

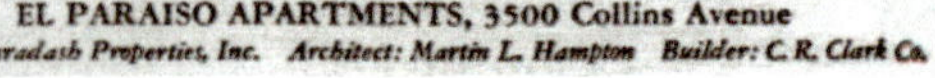

EL PARAISO APARTMENTS, 3500 Collins Avenue
aradash Properties, Inc. Architect: Martin L. Hampton Builder: C. R. Clark Co.

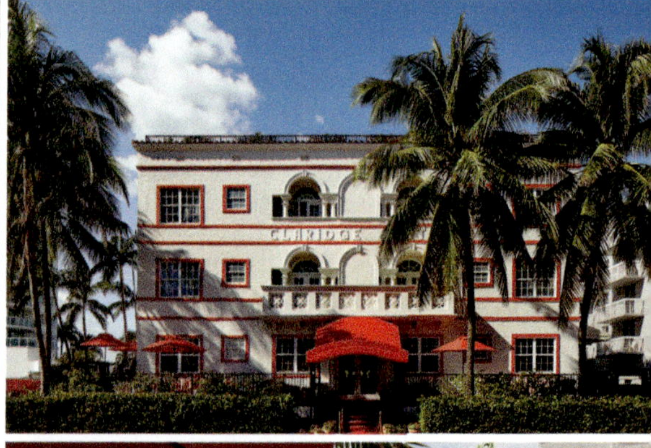

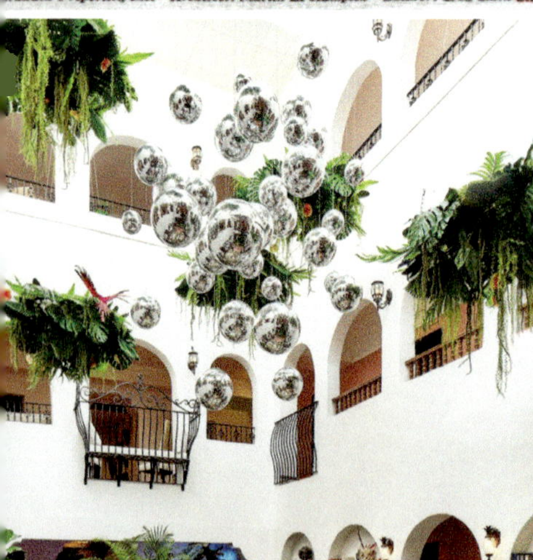

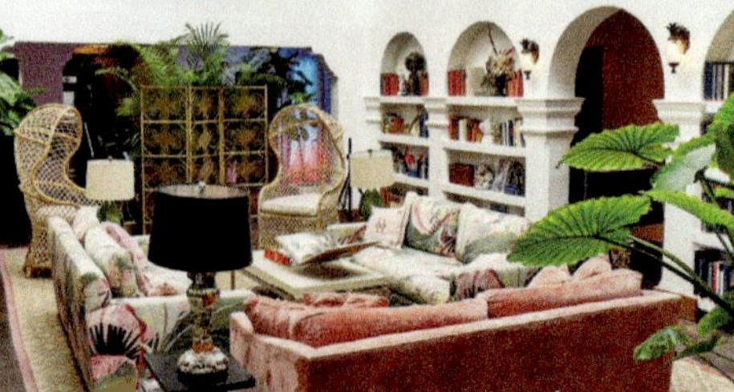

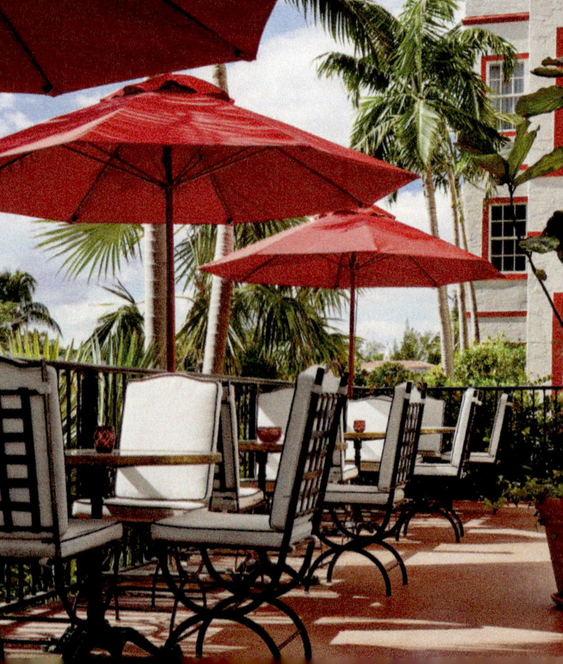

Casa Faena

Miami Beach

Opened: 1928 | Rooms: 38

What makes it special: This Spanish-style hotel on Miami's Collins Avenue has a vibrant new life as part of the Faena District.

The 17 apartments and two hotel rooms were built in a Mediterranean style on Miami Beach's mid-beach and offered a homey stay for winter travelers. "Those who are accustomed to the finer things in life, who love to dwell in an atmosphere of beauty, will find the El Paraiso Apartments a residence that expresses their culture and refinement," read a 1930 ad in the *Miami Herald* for the spot. The building later became the Claridge Hotel. According to Historic Hotels of America, it was leased to the United States military during World War II. In 2013, the hotel joined the Faena District and opened as Casa Claridge a year later. The spot is now known as Casa Faena and features an updated version of Miami Beach's iconic flair.

If you visit: About 30 minutes down Miami Beach to South Beach, there's another iconic hotel that once was an iconic home. The Villa Casa Casuarina was once the home of renowned fashion designer Gianni Versace. It's now a hotel and a restaurant. Make reservations at Gianni's for a look inside.

3500 Collins Ave.
Miami Beach, Florida 33140

faena.com/casa-faena

Top: Courtesy of State Library and Archives of Florida. *Middle left:* 1931, *Miami News. All other photos:* Courtesy of Casa Faena

Top and middle right: Courtesy of State Library and Archives of Florida. Bottom left: Courtesy of Kristen Hare. Bottom right: Courtesy of Tampa-Hillsborough Public Library System

Safety Harbor Resort and Spa

Safety Harbor

Opened: 1929 | Rooms: 172

What makes it special: Built on Espiritu Santo Springs, the hotel and its spa use the water thought for hundreds of years to offer healing qualities.

In the nail salon at the Safety Harbor Resort and Spa, you'll find glimpses of what's made this spot popular for hundreds of years. The Espiritu Santo Springs can be seen here, through clear cutouts in the floor, bubbling away like they have since some of Florida's earliest people discovered them. The space was first inhabited by Tocobaga Indians. In 1539, Spanish explorer Hernando de Soto arrived and thought he'd found the fountain of youth. Early hotels that made use of the springs include Pipkin Mineral Wells Hotel, Springs Hotel, and the Espiritu Santo Springs Hotel. In 1936, Dr. A. U. Jansik, an Austrian native, bought and renovated the springs and sanatorium. The spot became later the Safety Harbor Resort and Mineral Springs when it was bought and run by Dr. S. H. Baranoff in 1945. The doctor, a native of Kiev, Ukraine (then Russia), came to Safety Harbor from New York seeking warmer weather. By that time, the property was a rehabilitation sanatorium for alcoholics, according to his 1977 obituary in the *St. Petersburg Times*. Dr. Baranoff believed in natural healing, and he also believed in community. He was an active member of the Jewish community and donated the land where Safety Harbor's library still sits. Today, the Safety Harbor Resort and Spa are part of Wyndham's Trademark Collection. A short walk away, Baranoff is remembered through the enormous live oak named after him at nearby Baranoff Park.

If you visit: Stay for a spa treatment and you can enjoy the spa's pool, hot tub, saunas, steam rooms and plunge pools for the day.

105 N Bayshore Dr.
Safety Harbor, Florida 34695

safetyharborspa.com

1930s

AND

1940s

Many of the swankier tourist lodgings operated at a loss during the 1930s, opening up space for a new kind of entrepreneur—the moms and pops.

People were still relocating to Florida, said historian Joseph Vars, and they started taking advantage of underdevelopment, adding apartment hotels and cottages.

During World War II, many of the big and grand hotels in the state were requisitioned by the US military. It had an unexpected upside.

"That was the best promotion for Florida that the state could ask for at the time," Vars said. "The amount of people who relocated to Florida following World War II can be traced directly back to being trained here during the early portions of the war."

Those grand hotels where people stayed for the winter started to be replaced by more modest lodgings where people spent a week or two, said Historic Hotels of America's Lawrence Horwitz. And many of the new Floridians still wanted to vacation here.

"Florida's starting to be a year-round place to live," he said. "The growth of the citrus industry is very important to drawing people there year-round. Air conditioning is now affordable. Construction is affordable. And those people now living within are looking for places to vacation."

'Tween Waters Island Resort & Spa

Captiva Island

Opened: 1931 | Rooms: 135

What makes it special: The name says it all.

'Tween Waters Inn's early ads read "On the Gulf - On the Bay." The 1931 inn on Captiva Island offered both. This inn, built by F. Bowman and Grace B. Price, used the island's first schoolhouse as their restaurant. A few years later, famed editorial cartoonist J. N. "Ding" Darling visited the inn and wrote "We do not dress for dinner and the fishing is marvelous. I hope no one else ever finds it . . . " Over time, the couple added cottages, and both the inn and Captiva became a favorite respite for northerners. In 1976, one of those northerners, Tony Lapi, bought the inn and made it the first member of the Rochester Resorts family. In 2022, the inn closed briefly due to damage from Hurricane Ian. The original schoolhouse that anchored the inn still stands. Today, it's the Old Captiva House restaurant and includes a selection of Ding's 1940s illustrations.

If you visit: 'Tween Waters Inn is classic old Florida, and the Bubble Room restaurant is classic wacky Florida. Visit Boops, the restaurant's soda fountain and dessert stop, for a slice of the famed orange crunch cake.

15951 Captiva Dr.
Captiva, Florida 33924

tween-waters.com

Courtesy of 'Tween Waters Inn

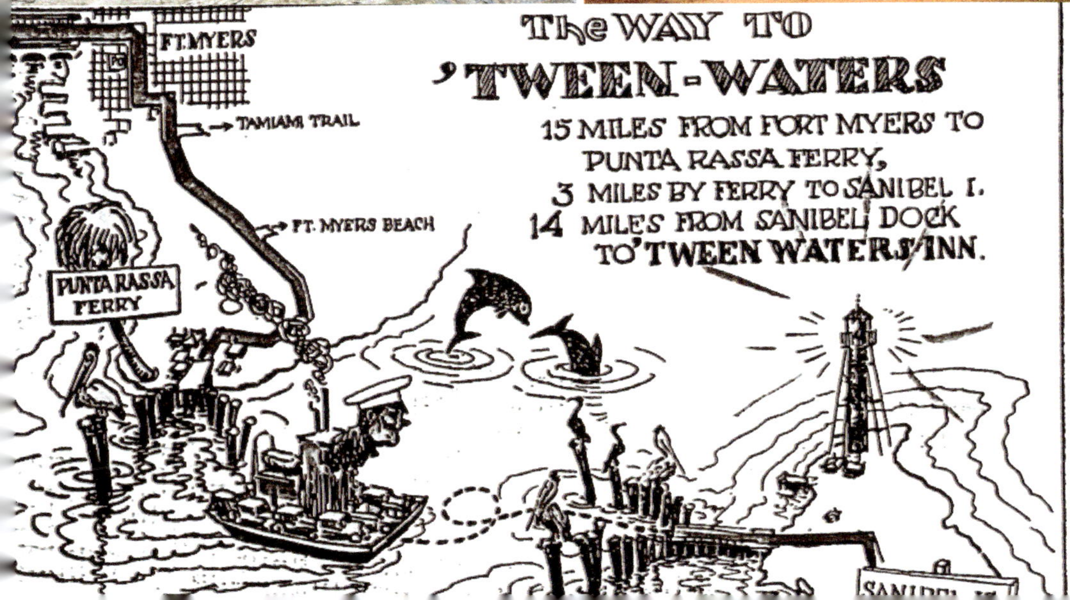

The WAY TO
'TWEEN-WATERS

15 MILES FROM FORT MYERS TO
PUNTA RASSA FERRY,
3 MILES BY FERRY TO SANIBEL I.
14 MILES FROM SANIBEL DOCK
TO 'TWEEN WATERS INN.

FT. MYERS
TAMIAMI TRAIL
FT. MYERS BEACH
PUNTA RASSA
FERRY

THE SAVOY HOTEL AND BEACH CLUB

MIAMI BEACH

OPENED: 1935 | ROOMS: 75

WHAT MAKES IT SPECIAL: THE TWO POOLS AT THIS SPOT ARE PICTURE-PERFECT AND MAKE FOR PERFECT PICTURES.

London, New York, and Florence all have their own Savoy hotels, but only Miami Beach has its own Savoy that's also an Art Deco palace. As the Savoy stands today, it's also actually two historic hotels. Built in the mid-1930s, the Savoy Plaza opened on Ocean Drive in Miami Beach. This new hotel was smaller than the grand ones built just a decade earlier, according to Historic Hotels of America, in response to the Great Depression and the Great Miami Hurricane. The Savoy was designed by architect V. M. Neillenbogen. The second hotel that's now part of the Savoy is the 1930s' Hotel Arlington, designed by Albert Anis. The two were combined in 2012 and underwent a big restoration in 2020. The Savoy is owned by New York–based Allied Partners. Visit today and you'll find ocean views, playful Miami decor, two pools, and a library.

IF YOU VISIT: CHECK OUT ANOTHER ICONIC MIAMI NEIGHBORHOOD—WYNWOOD. THIS NEIGHBORHOOD, FULL OF SHOPS, BARS, AND RESTAURANTS, IS A STREET ART MARVEL.

425 OCEAN DR.
MIAMI BEACH, FLORIDA 33139

savoy-miami.com

Top and bottom right: Courtesy of The Savoy
Bottom left: Courtesy of State Library and Archives of Florida

Driftwood Resort

Vero Beach

Opened: 1937 | Rooms: 100

What makes it special: This hotel includes the eclectic antiques collections of the original owner, Waldo Sexton.

The Driftwood Inn was first built as a sort of scavenged private beach home but soon turned into an inn. Built of cypress and pecky cypress, it opened in 1937. Owner Waldo Sexton was considered one of the area's early pioneers and an eccentric one at that. He owned McKee Botanical Garden, Ocean Grill, and other popular Vero Beach spots. Sexton, an antiques lover, filled his businesses with his finds, including a large collection of bells. "The Driftwood affectionately calls this the 'Menagerie of Monstrosities,'" the hotel says on its website. Over time, more wings were added to the inn, and in 1980, part of the Driftwood was converted into a time-share. In 2004, the Driftwood suffered after two hurricanes hit. It reopened one year later. The Driftwood is today what Sexton first started building, "a unique seaside hotel built partially of driftwood and other relics of the sea by Waldo E. Sexton as part of his wood collecting hobby," read the back of a postcard from sometime between the 1930s and '40s. "The original design of the building, together with the unusual furniture and many collectors' items which it contains, make Driftwood a mecca for the curios."

If you visit: Eat at Ocean Grill, Waldo Sexton's 1940s restaurant, which doubled as an officers' club during World War II.

3150 Ocean Dr.
Vero Beach, Florida 32963

verobeachdriftwood.com

Top: Courtesy of Driftwood Resort
Bottom left: 1966, courtesy of State Library and Archives of Florida
Bottom right: 1951, courtesy of State Library and Archives of Florida

The Lodge at Wakulla Springs

Crawfordville

Opened: 1937 | Rooms: 27

What makes it special: The ceiling of the lodge holds heart cypress planks painted in detail with various types of folk art by the German painter Piplack, thought to be the last court painter for Kaiser Wilhelm.

Florida and Florida hotels are often the settings for Hollywood. The Lodge at Wakulla Springs has been that setting many times. The spring here has appeared in films including the 1940s' *Tarzan* and the 1950s' *The Creature from the Black Lagoon*. But the lodge itself has an even richer history. Built by Edward Ball, the lodge opened in 1937 away from the bustle of tourist destinations, beaches, and cities. During World War II, the lodge was used to house men from Camp Gordon Johnston and their families, according to the hotel. Inside today, it is nearly as magnificent as it is outside. Built in a mix of Spanish-Moorish and Art Deco styles, the lodge has heart cypress, marble, and ironwork. You can dine at the Edward Ball Dining Room and try the navy bean soup, which has been served at the hotel since it opened. Visit the original elevator. Meet Old Joe the Alligator, an 11-foot marvel preserved in the lobby. Head to the gift shop, where you can buy *Creature from the Black Lagoon* merchandise. And check out the soda fountain, which is reported to hold the world's longest marble bar at just over 70 feet. That space also holds what was Wakulla County's first post office.

If you visit: Head to the lodge's soda fountain and ask for the Ginger Yip, a yummy milkshake that the soda jerks are happy to enhance with a shot of bourbon.

550 Wakulla Park Dr.
Crawfordville, Florida 32327

thelodgeatwakullasprings.com

Top: Courtesy of Kristen Hare
All other photos: Courtesy of State Library and Archives of Florida

Seahorse Cottages

Treasure Island

Opened: 1939 | Rooms: five cottages and two suites

What makes it special: Built for beach renovations, the cottages stand out among tall motels and condos.

Old Florida still stands on a small stretch of Treasure Island. Here, five bright cottages have weathered hurricanes, time, and development. The wooden structures were built in 1938 as temporary homes for members of the Army Corps of Engineers during a beach renovation, according to current owners. In 1939, they became holiday rentals and were owned and run by Earle Cobb. Later known as the Jerrell Apartments and Cottages, the property was sold to Coleman Kilmartin, a World War II navy veteran who came to Florida in 1947, according to the *St. Petersburg Times,* and later to Roseanne Petit, a former English teacher. A grocery store, Treasure Island's first, once occupied the property's Gulf Boulevard storefront. The Seahorse Cottages are surrounded by tall hotels and condos. In 2002, community members fought against new development proposals. The cottages have held their own, and in 2022, they got renovated to make the most of their simple spaces and phenomenal ocean views.

If you visit: Explore John's Pass Village, a waterfront fishing village with shops, restaurants, and bars.

10356 Gulf Blvd.
Treasure Island, Florida 33706

seahorsebeachfront.itrip.co

Bottom right: Courtesy of Barbara Driscoll, president, Treasure Island Historical Society
All others: Courtesy of Kristen Hare

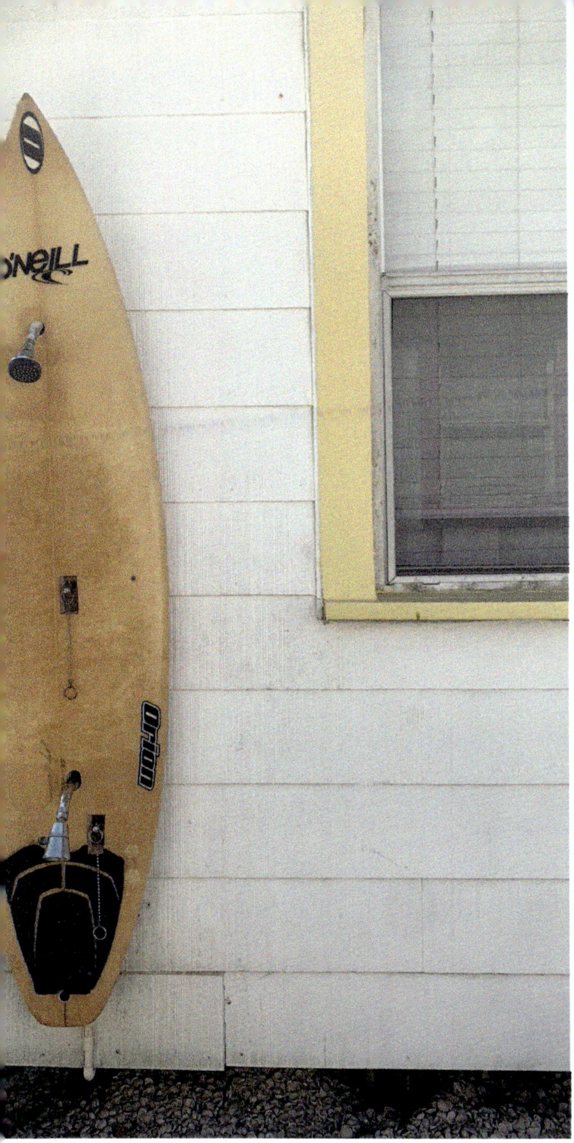

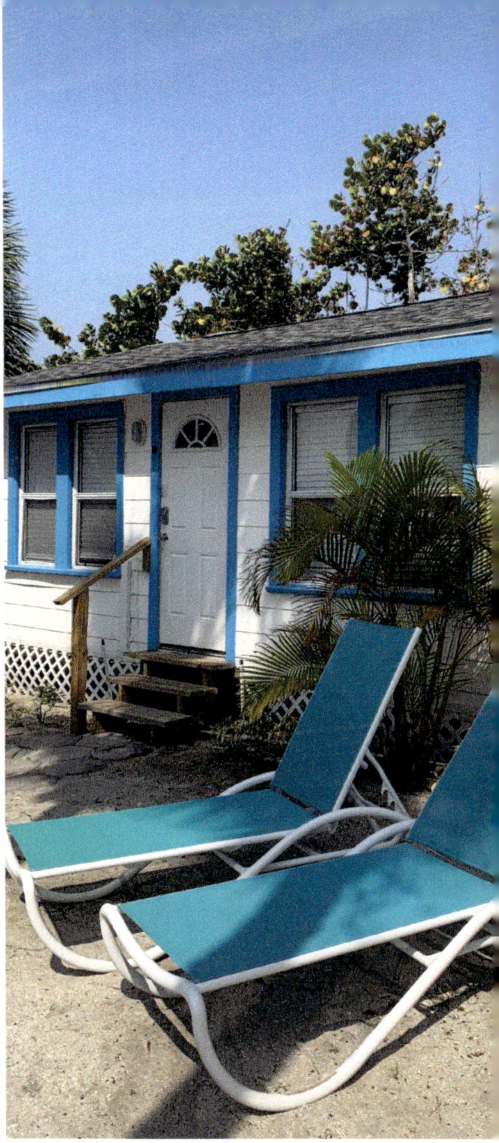

SEAHORSE
COTTAGES & APARTMENTS
ON TREASURE ISLAND BEAC

TOM AND ROSEANNE PETIT
OWNERS
TREASURE ISLAND, FLORIDA

THE BALFOUR HOTEL

MIAMI BEACH

OPENED: 1940 | ROOMS: 82

WHAT MAKES IT SPECIAL: THE ART DECO BUILDING WAS BUILT IN A U SHAPE SO ALL THE ROOMS HAVE VIEWS OF THE COURTYARD.

This Miami Beach hotel opened in 1940, named after the Earl of Balfour, according to the *Miami News,* the "British statesman who sponsored the Balfour act, creating Palestine as the national home of the Jewish race." The hotel was designed in the Art Deco style by Croatian architect Anton Skislewicz, according to Historic Hotels of America. The Miami Design Preservation League called Skislewicz important "to the fabric of Miami Beach's Art Deco history. Skislewicz was the architect of many Art Deco apartment buildings, private homes and hotels throughout the 1930s and the early 40s including the Breakwater Hotel (1939), the Plymouth Hotel (1940), Ocean Surf (1940), the Kenmore Hotel (1936) and the Lord Balfour Hotel (1940)." Over the years, the hotel has had different owners and clientele, from Hasidic Jews to European clubgoers.

IF YOU VISIT: DOUBLE-DECKER TOURS OF MIAMI GET YOU TO THE MAJOR SPOTS IN THE CITY WITH STOPS IN LITTLE HAVANA AND MIAMI BEACH. BONUS: YOU DON'T HAVE TO FIGHT MIAMI TRAFFIC YOURSELF.

350 OCEAN DR.
MIAMI BEACH, FLORIDA 33139

thebalfourmiamibeach.com

Middle left: Courtesy of Wikimedia Commons
All other photos: Courtesy of the Balfour Hotel

er of 4th and Ocean Drive
HOTEL
LORD BALFOUR
Lord Balfour

Streamline Hotel

Daytona Beach

Opened: 1941 | Rooms: 44

What makes it special: NASCAR was born here.

The Streamline Hotel opened in Daytona Beach in 1941 with "a quiet cool coffee shop and a roof garden for dancing," reported an *Orlando Sentinel* story from that year. Open all year and offering a sleek Art Deco style, the Streamline soon became famous for something else. In 1947, Bill France Sr. and other community members started a three-day meeting on the Streamline's rooftop about Daytona Beach's popular beachfront racing. The result of their work—The National Association for Stock Car Auto Racing, or NASCAR. "The purpose of this association is to unite all stock car racing under one set of rules," France said, "to set up a benevolent fund and a national point standing system whereby only one stock car driver will be crowned national champion." NASCAR's first official race took place two months later. The Streamline got a makeover in 2014 and was featured on the Travel Channel's hotel makeover show *Hotel Impossible*. During renovations,

workers discovered a sealed tunnel that led to the beach, thought to be the preferred path for moonshiners, according to the hotel. In 2017, the hotel reopened. Today, it's owned by an investment group out of New York and continues telling the story of NASCAR's birth.

IF YOU VISIT: EVEN IF YOU DON'T LIKE NASCAR, THE DAYTONA SPEEDWAY TOUR IS WORTH YOUR TIME. GET TO KNOW THE HISTORY AND TRADITIONS OF THE SPEEDWAY, RIDE A TROLLEY ON THE GROUNDS, AND ENJOY THE QUIET OF THE EMPTY STADIUM.

140 S ATLANTIC AVE.
DAYTONA BEACH, FLORIDA 32118

streamlinehotel.com

Top row: Courtesy of State Library and Archives of Florida. *Bottom left:* Courtesy of Kristen Hare. *Bottom middle and right:* Courtesy of Streamline Hotel

The Betsy Hotel

Miami Beach

Opened: 1942 Rooms: 130

What makes it special: Among rows of Art Deco gems, the Betsy is both an example of Florida Georgian architecture and, with the Orb that connects it to another building, an example of an evolving Miami.

The Betsy Ross Hotel in Miami has had decades of news-making since opening. Construction started in 1941. When it opened one year later, it was leased to the US Army to station troops during World War II. By 1943, the "unusually attractive colonial structure" was sold to new owners, according to a *Miami Herald* article from the time. In 1948, the Libman family became the hotel's owners. In 1952, the property drew angry White protesters when it was among the Miami Beach hotels to host an integrated education conference, the *Herald* reported. In 1972, the National Women's Political Caucus hosted meetings at the hotel. In 2003, the Betsy was renovated. It became the Besty Hotel South Beach in 2006. In 2009, the hotel got another big renovation. It later expanded into the former Carlton Hotel, adding a sky bridge, known as the Orb, that's as remarkable and distinct as the Betsy itself. The Betsy is owned by Jonathan Plutzik and his wife, Lesley Goldwasser.

If you visit: Make sure to see the Orb; the Art Deco Carlton Room, which was the former lobby of the Carlton; and the Poetry Rail, which celebrates poets who contributed to Miami, including Langston Hughes.

1440 Ocean Dr.
Miami, Florida 33139

thebetsyhotel.com

Courtesy of The Betsy

Cabbage Key Inn

Cabbage Key

Opened: 1944 | Rooms: Six rooms and seven cottages

What makes it special: Only reachable by boat, this spot has historic charm and stunning views.

The spot that's now known as Cabbage Key was originally home to the Calusa native people until the mid-1700s. In 1936, Alan and Gratia Rinehart bought the island and started building their home atop the island's shell midden, which the Calusa built. The original property included the main house, a boathouse, two cottages, and a water tower. One of the cottages, known as the Doll House, was built as a playhouse for the couple's daughters. The island also served as a field station for the study of tarpon. In 1939, the island, then known as Palmetto Key, was sold after Gratia's death. In 1944, Jan and Larry Stults took over the island and began converting it into an inn. Visitors found a laid-back spot with adventures including dinners aboard a boat and art lessons from Larry, an artist, according to the inn. The island had two more owners after the Stultses, and, in 1971, people started tacking dollar bills up in the inn's bar, a tradition that still continues and has earned

Left: Courtesy of Maxwell MacKenzie. *Right*: Courtesy of Cabbage Key Inn

the spot the nickname "Dollar Bill Bar." In 1976, Rob and Phyllis Wells bought the island and the property has been in the family since. The Wellses also own nearby Tarpon Lodge on Pine Island. Ignore the power boats and tourists taking selfies and the island must look much like it did early on, with charming cottages, including the Doll House, and six guest rooms. The original water tower is still standing, and the views from the top are postcard-worthy.

IF YOU VISIT: TRY THE FRESH CATCH AT THE POPULAR CABBAGE KEY RESTAURANT AND FINISH IT OFF WITH THE INN'S SIGNATURE FROZEN KEY LIME PIE.

CABBAGE KEY, FLORIDA

cabbagekey.com

Photos: Courtesy of Cabbage Key Inn

Keystone Motel

St. Pete Beach

Opened: 1945 | Rooms: 33

What makes it special: This classic St. Pete Beach motel is still owned and operated by the same family who built it.

In the 1920s, Italian immigrant Bruno Reitano and his daughter, Mary, took the train from Maryland to St. Petersburg for a healing getaway. They ended up at Pass-a-Grille Beach and found, instead, miles of possibilities. In 1945, Reitano moved his family to Florida and built the Keystone Motel, which he ran with his two oldest daughters. When her kids finished high school, daughter Mary Falkenstein joined them. By 1963, the family opened the Steak Pit, a restaurant with a make-it-yourself salad bar. For years, the motel included a lounge with live music and dancing nightly. Reitano, who loved animals, once kept a pet alligator under the motel's stairs. After his death in 1964, Falkenstein and her family took over the business. She was known to her community, customers, and family as Nanny. Though she worked seven days a week steps from the beach, Falkenstein never learned to swim. She had a favorite saying that might explain that: "Hard work will never kill you, but laziness

Left: Courtesy of Kristen Hare. *Right:* Courtesy of Keystone Motel

will." Nanny worked at the Keystone until her death at 99. The fourth generation now runs the beachfront motel, but Nanny's still at the spot that's now a Florida Heritage site. A mural of her covers one of the building's exterior walls. She had another saying about work and life on Pass-a-Grille Beach: "No two sunsets are ever the same."

IF YOU VISIT: HEAD OVER TO THE FAMILY'S HURRICANE SEAFOOD RESTAURANT A FEW DOORS DOWN AND CLIMB UP TO THE ROOFTOP DECK FOR A COLD DRINK AND GREAT VIEWS.

801 GULF WAY
ST. PETE BEACH, FLORIDA 33706

keystonemotel.com

Top: Courtesy of Keystone Motel. *Bottom:* Courtesy of Kristen Hare

Cheeca Lodge & Spa

Islamorada

Opened: 1946 | Rooms: 243

What makes it special: Some hotels are named after great men, some after royal women. This one was a 1960s "Brangelina."

The spot where Cheeca Lodge & Spa sits today has been the spot where other hotels once sat, too. It started with Casa Islamorado, which was soon renamed Islamorada Olney Inn and owned by Clara May Downey. In the early 1960s, the inn was destroyed by a hurricane. The property was next bought by Carl and Cynthia Twitchell (heiress to the A&P grocery store chain), who started rebuilding when a fire destroyed everything again, according to a *Palm Beach Post* story from 1962. They rebuilt and this time named the spot the Cheeca Lodge. "How did Cheeca get its name?" the *Miami Herald* asked that November. "Cynthia Twitchell's nickname is Chee and her husband's name is Carl, so they put the two together." The hotel had many owners over the years and closed again in 2009 after another fire, reopening 11 months later. It's currently owned by Northwood Investments. The Cheeca has long been a magnet for US presidents, from Harry S. Truman when the hotel on the property was the Olney Inn to George H.W. Bush at the Cheeca.

If you visit: The eclectic Rain Barrell Village offers shopping, food, art, and a 30-foot fiberglass lobster out front.

81801 Overseas Hwy.
Islamorada, Florida 33036

cheeca.com

ANT TO GET AWAY FROM IT ALL?

Clara May Downey's

Olney Inn

Then come to the new Olney Inn, famous for food and complete relaxation. Hospitality unlimited, restfulness unmatched in a secluded and vast coconut grove on the Atlantic Ocean at Islamorada. If you *must do something*, here too are the world famous bonefish flats, with charter boats and guides nearby.

ne Matacumbe 3511 or Write P.O. Box 187, Islamorada, Fla.

Top left: Courtesy of State Library and Archives of Florida. *Top right and bottom:* Courtesy of Cheeca Lodge and Spa. *Middle left:* Ad from Ft. Lauderdale News, 1954

The Sands

Treasure Island

Opened: 1947 | Rooms: 34

What makes it special: This motel offers neon, charm, and a short stroll to the beach.

The Sands of Treasure Island opened in 1947 during a hotel and motel building boom on the Gulf of Mexico. Built by Herbert Dowling, the mid-century Sands Motel was Treasure Island's first concrete building. That stretch of Gulf Boulevard soon became known as Treasure Island's Golden Mile. A color brochure for the Sands promised a heated pool, carpeting, kitchens, and Beautyrest mattresses. Dowling served as Treasure Island's mayor before the city consolidated. He followed up with other properties, including the Surf, another mid-century motel. It survived until 2005, when it was torn down. With bright yellow doors and a glowing neon sign, the Sands still has a pool, shuffleboard, and tons of charm. It's also maintained some loyal guests, including an Illinois couple who has vacationed there for more than 55 years.

If you visit: Head into St. Petersburg and visit another distinct spot, the Salvador Dalí Museum, which features the artist's iconic works, a wish tree, an Avant Garden, and a magnificent gift shop, all in a building unlike any you've likely ever been.

**11800 Gulf Blvd.
Treasure Island, Florida 33706**

sandsoftreasureisland.com

Top left and bottom: Courtesy of Kristen Hare. *Top right and middle left:* Courtesy of The Sands of Treasure Island

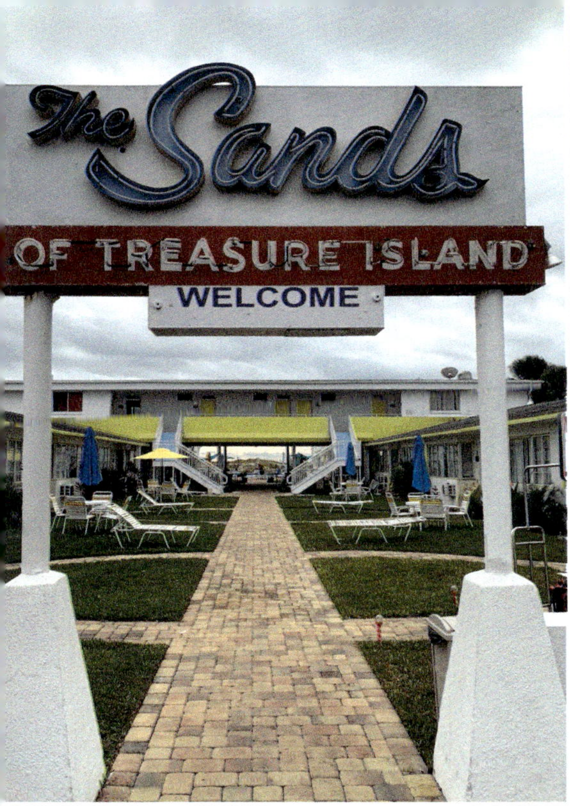
The Sands
OF TREASURE ISLAND
WELCOME

The Sands
OF TREASURE ISLAND
11800 GULF BLVD. ST. PETERSBURG, FLA.
PHONE 361-1771

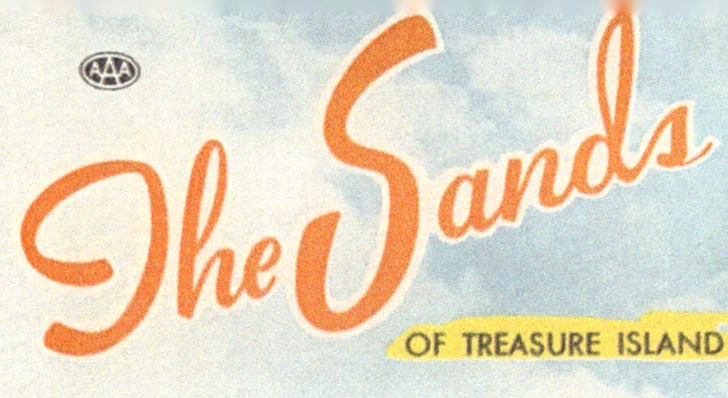

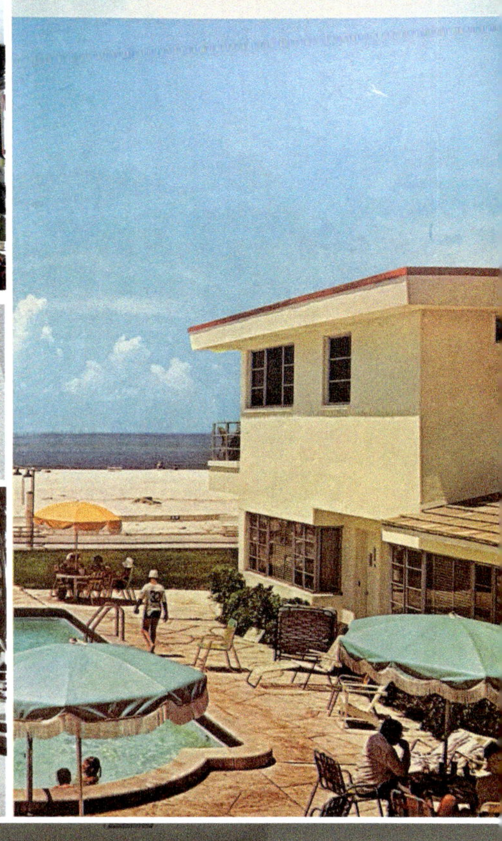

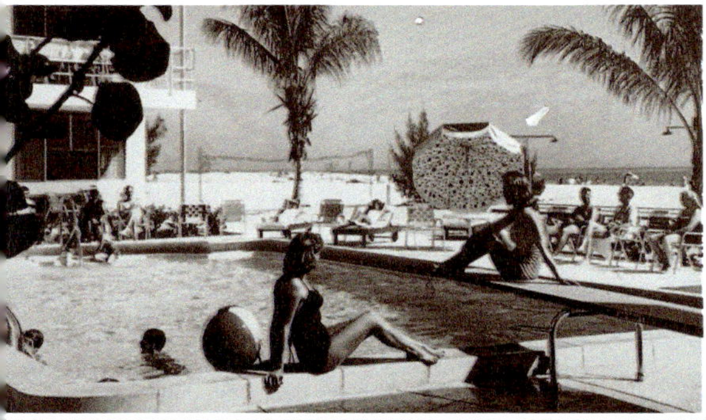

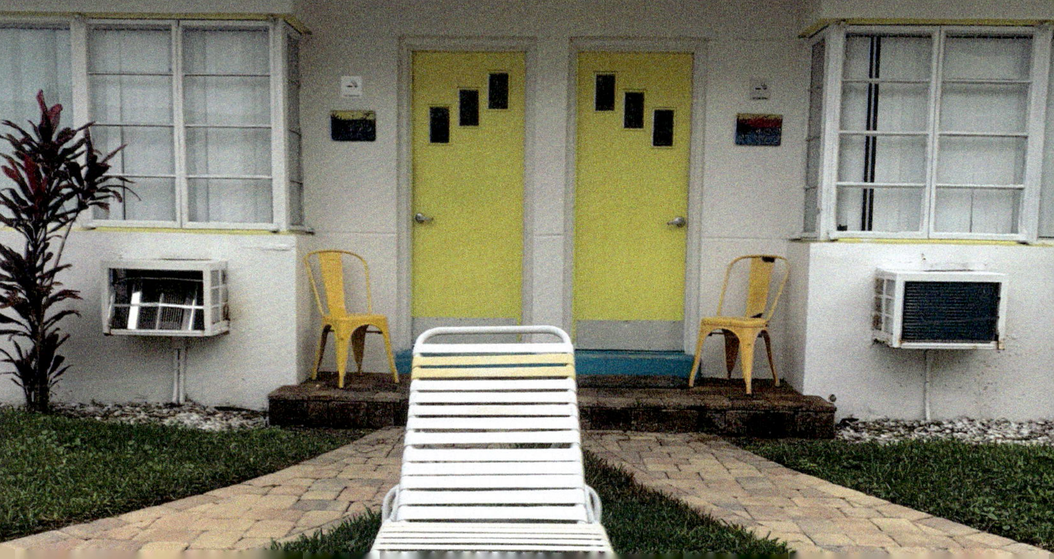

COLONY HOTEL

PALM BEACH

OPENED: 1947 | ROOMS: 93

WHAT MAKES IT SPECIAL: THE "PINK PARADISE" IS A PRIME EXAMPLE OF A HISTORIC FLORIDA HOTEL THAT HAS EVOLVED WITH THE TIMES. IT WAS NOT ORIGINALLY PINK, BUT IT'S A PERFECT ADDITION TO FLORIDA'S PINK HOTEL COLLECTION.

From the time in opened in 1947, the Colony Hotel was known for its looks. "This new hotel, whose deep mulberry facade with white trim, is a prominent addition to the landscape at this point," the *Palm Beach Post* reported. "(It) presents an interesting tie-up between the resort's hotel life of today and that of yesterday . . . " Past the tourism boom at the start of the century and the challenges of the Great Depression, the Colony was at the time a more modern take on tourist lodgings, including by offering air-conditioning. The hotel, which had a bar called the Bird Cage, was a glamour magnet throughout the decades, drawing new owners and famous guests. Those guests included the Duke and Duchess of Windsor. And the Kennedys came by for dinners in the 1960s. In 2001, the hotel added a supper club with a cabaret. In 2014, it got a $9 million makeover and the exterior joined the ranks of Florida's famed pink hotels. New owners, the Wetenhalls, took over care of the Colony in 2016, and from 2018 to 2020, the hotel got its most luxe and fun makeover yet. Visit today and you'll find delightful

Bottom left: Courtesy of Carmel Brantley. *Bottom right:* Courtesy of The Colony Hotel

interiors wrapped in bright wallpapers with eclectic furniture and decor. Fittingly, Johnnie Brown, the pet monkey of famed South Florida architect Addison Mizner, is now the Colony's mascot. It's a perfectly playful nod to the past.

IF YOU VISIT: MAKE THE TIME TO DISCOVER WHITEHALL, RAILROAD MAGNATE HENRY FLAGLER'S ONCE-GRAND MANSION THAT'S NOW THE HENRY MORRISON FLAGLER MUSEUM. STEPPING INTO THE GLASS-ENCLOSED PAVILION WILL GIVE YOU A PRETTY GOOD SENSE OF WHAT LIFE WAS LIKE FOR THOSE ON TOP DURING THE GILDED AGE.

155 HAMMON AVE.
PALM BEACH, FLORIDA 33480

thecolonypalmbeach.com

Top left: Courtesy of Carmel Brantley. *Top right:* Courtesy of Lesley Unruh
Bottom: Courtesy of The Colony Hotel

The Wellborn

Orlando

Opened: 1947 | Rooms: 20

What makes it special: You can see this darling pink Art Deco hotel when you stop by The Wellborn's restaurant next door for brunch or drinks.

Orlando's pink Art Deco hotel opened as the Wellborn Apartment Hotel along Lake Lucerne in 1947. It was named after developer Wellborn C. Phillips, according to the *Orlando Sentinel.* Phillips' legacy extends around the city. He built much of the housing there in the 1940s and '50s and the Rio Pinar Country Club in the 1950s. "Wellborn Phillips is a man's man," the *Orlando Sentinel* fawningly reported in 1957. "He likes boating, fishing and storytelling (and has a wealth of yarns). He likes a drink (double martinis, dry) and belly laughs." Along with the Norment-Parry House, thought to be Orlando's oldest home, and the 1917 I.W. Phillips House, the 20-room hotel became part of the Courtyard at Lake Lucerne complex in the 1980s, according to press clippings. In 2019, it all became the Wellborn. Today there's a restaurant and bar and multiple places to stay, including the original Wellborn hotel, now managed by Sonder.

If you visit: You can see this darling pink Art Deco hotel when you stop by The Wellborn's restaurant next door for brunch or drinks.

211 N Lucerne Cir. E
Orlando, Florida 32801

thewellbornorlando.com

Top left, top right, bottom right: Courtesy of Kristen Hare. *Middle left and bottom left:* Courtesy of State Library and Archives of Florida

BEACH HAVEN

ST. PETE BEACH

OPENED: 1949 | ROOMS: 18

WHAT MAKES IT SPECIAL: THE BRIGHT PINK MOTEL STILL HAS ITS ORIGINAL DECORATIVE MEDALLIONS, INCLUDING SHIPS, A PINK FLAMINGO AND A SHOREBIRD.

In February of 1949, Harry and Gay Huston bought the Gulf Boulevard motel they'd previously visited with their family on a trip from Pennsylvania. By that September, they were building a new property across the street and called both Fairview Manor. The couple ran the modest beachfront property for 25 years. It later became the Fairview Motel, then New Beach Haven and now Beach Haven. Today, the bright pink and blue spot is a true throwback to the mid-century motels that once lined Florida beaches. Beach Haven is now flanked by two high-rises, but inside the corridor between the two buildings, looking past the pool to the long stretch of beach, it's easy to imagine what vacations were like for visitors here 75 years ago and why it's still a holiday spot today.

IF YOU VISIT: GRAB BREAKFAST AT ANOTHER LOCAL LANDMARK, THE SEAHORSE RESTAURANT ON PASS-A-GRILLE. THE LINE THAT'S LIKELY TO BE AROUND THE BLOCK IS WORTH THE WAIT.

4980 GULF BLVD.
ST. PETE BEACH, FLORIDA 33706

beachhavenvillas.com

Top left, top right and bottom right: Courtesy of Kristen Hare. *Middle left:* Courtesy of Beach Haven. *Bottom left:* Courtesy of State Library and Archives of Florida

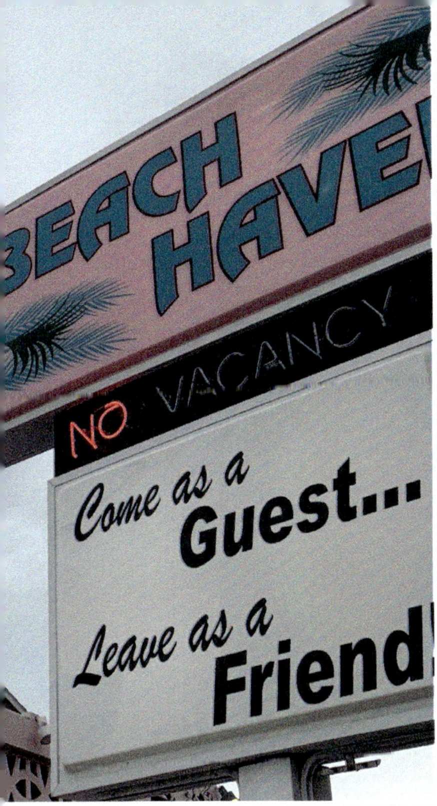
BEACH HAVE
NO VACANCY
Come as a Guest...
Leave as a Friend!

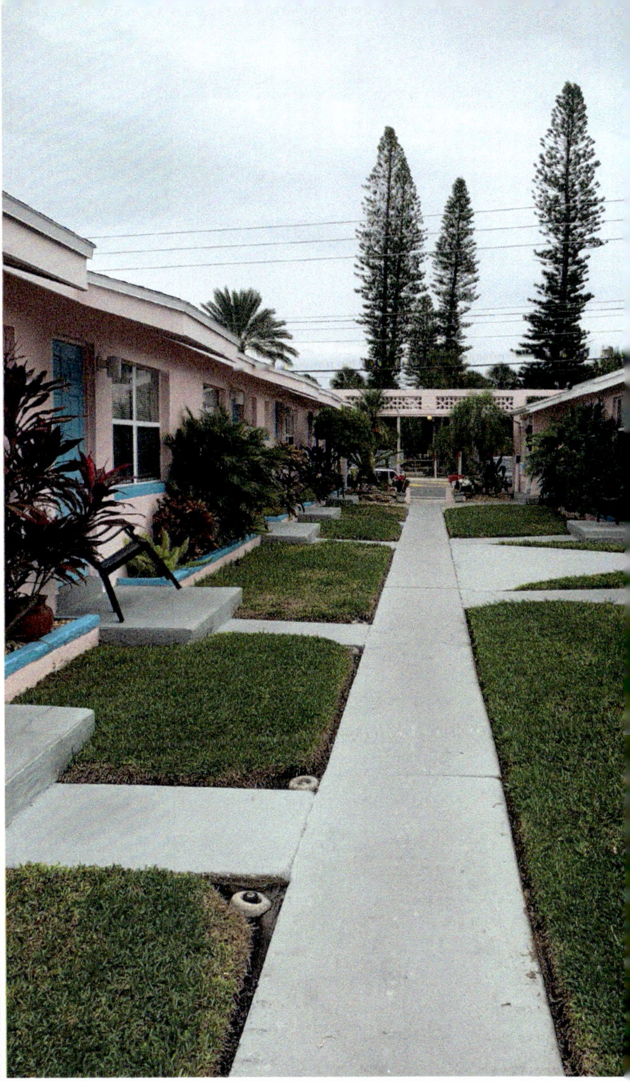

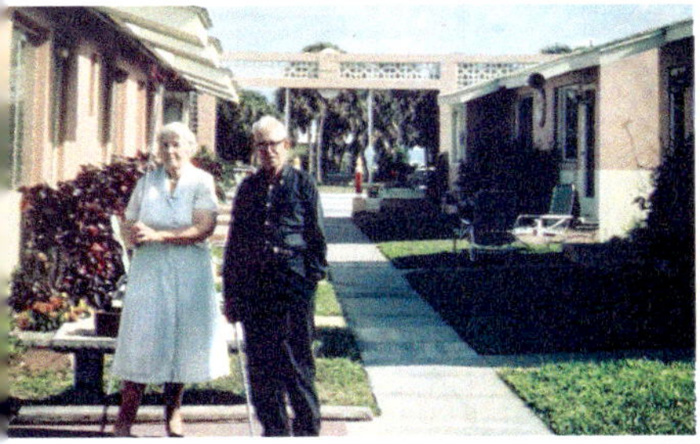

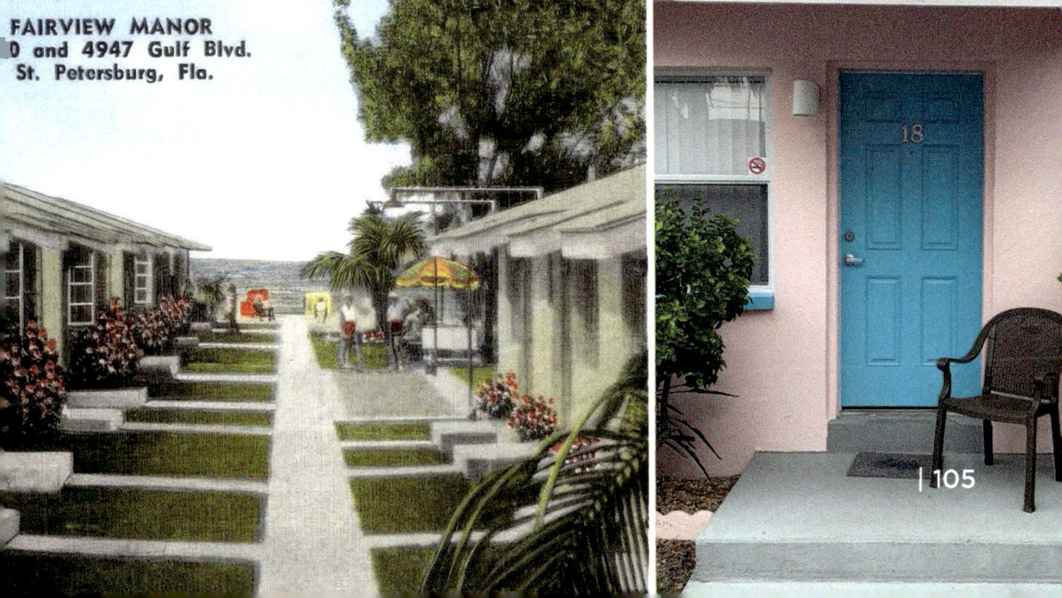

FAIRVIEW MANOR
0 and 4947 Gulf Blvd.
St. Petersburg, Fla.

18

1950s

Postwar Florida offered northerners something new.

"The concept of fun in the sun started to be considered in this time," said historian Joseph Vars.

The bikini had recently been invented. And for the first time, there was something new in Florida drawing tourists—the beaches.

"That was a whole other creation of the image of Florida," said historian Rodney Kite-Powell, "all those little mom-and-pop hotels and motels. If you ask somebody in Wisconsin what is Florida? That is Florida. That's coming down on a vacation and staying in one of those little places on the beach. And that really went a long way toward creating the image of Florida."

It wasn't like the regal days of palatial palaces anymore. Everyone had their favorite spot, Kite-Powell said.

"It's a more democratic version of that Florida tourist experience."

With the advent of color TV, images of bright beach balls and colorful new motels you could drive to added to Floria's roadside culture allure. Many of the hotels that still stand from this era were playful. One was built to look like a giant ship. Another like something out of the Wild West. Architects were also showing their skills in this decade through thoroughly modern designs we now recognize as mid-century.

Moonrise Resort

Floral City

Opened: 1950 | Rooms: five cabins

What makes it special: This old fish camp sits on Lake Tsala Apopka, which is known for abundant fishing and catching.

Moonrise Fish Camp started the way a lot of Florida tourist spots do—when northerners came down and made it their home. John and Anna Grimes purchased the spot in 1950 and built four cabins, according to the hotel. They lived in one of them with their children. The quaint fish camp with epic views had many owners over the years. By 1961, it was known as Moonrise Resort. It expanded with a mobile home park and made regular headlines for the big fish visitors caught in the lake. In 1986, Mike and Sue Ellen Friddle bought and cared for the space until they sold it in 2018. Since, the property has been owned by Birch Realty. Today, Moonrise has five cabins and an RV park. The resort has hosted generations of families since opening and is home to at least one man's ashes. His 2023 obituary explained "Some of his ashes will be spread over what he considered his favorite place in the

Courtesy of Kristen Hare

world, Moonrise Resort in Floral City on Lake Tsala Apopka, where he enjoyed many childhood vacations and adult fishing trips. Goodbye, little brother. You left us too early. We still had fish yet left to catch."

IF YOU VISIT: HEAD TO 90-SOMETHING-YEAR-OLD FERRIS GROVES, A ROADSIDE SHOP OPEN IN THE WINTER MONTHS, FOR ALL OF THE FRESH FRUIT THE AREA IS KNOWN FOR AND A DARN GOOD STRAWBERRY SHORTCAKE.

8801 E MOONRISE LN., LOT 18
FLORAL CITY, FLORIDA 34436

moonriseresort.com

Top left: Courtesy of State Library and Archives of Florida. *Top right, bottom right:* Courtesy of Kristen Hare. *Bottom left:* Ad from *Tampa Tribune*, 1963, courtesy of *Tampa Bay Times*

HOTEL DUVAL

TALLAHASSEE

OPENED: 1951 | ROOMS: 117

WHAT MAKES IT SPECIAL: THE ROOFTOP BAR OFFERS FANTASTIC VIEWS OF FLORIDA'S CAPITAL.

When the Hotel Duval opened in Tallahassee in 1951, it gave Florida's state capital three major hotels in town. The spot was named for Joseph W. Duval, who owned the property. When it opened, the walls were "wedgewood blue," the *Tallahassee Democrat* reported, and the chairs were red and chartreuse. The hotel was actually named for two men, J. W. Duval and "the first civilian governor of the Territory of Florida," William P. DuVal, the *Democrat* reported at the time. The hotel closed in 1969, and in 1970, it was gifted to Florida State University. In 2007, the property became a hotel once again and went through a $10 million renovation. Today it's part of Marriott's Autograph Collection. Visitors should head up to the eighth floor to the Level 8 Lounge for panoramic views of Tallahassee.

IF YOU VISIT: TOUR THE STATE CAPITOL BUILDING AND CHECK OUT THE OBSERVATORY ON THE 22ND FLOOR.

**415 N MONROE ST.
TALLAHASSEE, FLORIDA 32301**

marriott.com

Top left, bottom right: Courtesy of State Library and Archives of Florida. *Top right, middle and bottom left:* Courtesy of Marriott International

Hotel Duval
TALLAHASSEE, FLORIDA

OTEL
UVAL

Three Waters Resort and Marina

Islamorada

Opened: 1951 | Rooms: 214

What makes it special: The Tiki Bar at this spot is the birthplace of the rum runner. It's a historical tidbit worth tasting.

In 1951, the Holiday Isle Resort and Marina opened on Islamorada. When its Tiki Bar started serving drinks in 1969, it soon made cocktail history with the creation of the rum runner. "The Tiki has expanded in size over recent years," read a 1978 dispatch in the *Miami News,* "regrettable in terms of atmosphere since it is now frequently crowded with pink and peeling tourists . . . " In the early 2000s, the resort was expected to be demolished, but it was purchased and given a new name—the Postcard Inn, according to the *Miami Herald.* In 2017, it took a hit from Hurricane Irma. It reopened one year later. Today, the property and a few of its neighbors are part of the Islamorada Resort Collection, and in 2024, it got another new name—Three Waters Resort and Marina. This might be its swankiest incarnation yet. The new property includes what used to be Pelican Inn Resort and Marina, major renovations, and a refreshed Tiki Bar with the same drink that made it famous.

If you visit: From the resort, head over to Able's Tackle Box and General Store, order some bait and go feed the tarpon.

84001 Overseas Hwy.
Islamorada, Florida 33036

islamoradaresortcollection.com

Courtesy of State Library and Archives of Florida

Rod and Reel Resort

Anna Maria

Opened: 1952 | Rooms: Eight suites

What makes it special: With large, modern suites and spectacular views, the revived resort is a fitting new life for a historic space.

This special spot had a different name briefly, Emerald by the Sea, but for anyone who has visited Anna Maria Island, it will always be the Rod and Reel thanks to its immediate neighbor, the Rod & Reel Pier. This motel, on Anna Maria's north end, was built by local developer William E. Brier, who went on to serve as Anna Maria's mayor, according to news reports from the time. The hotel shares its name with one of Anna Maria's two iconic piers, which was built in 1947. Anna Maria has a much longer history, with regular visitors in the late 1800s and the establishment of a beach development company in 1911, according to the island's *Chamber of Commerce*. The motel, built in the era catering to road-tripping tourists, was owned and run by different people over the years. In 2015, it was bought by John and Suzette Buchan, who downsized the number of rooms in order to make it more family friendly with suites. Today, the Rod and Reel Resort offers visitors separate bedrooms and space to cook and relax. If they're too tired from a day in the water, they can walk next door to the pier for some fresh fish and amazing views.

If you visit: Stop for lunch or dinner at one of AMI's beloved restaurants, including the SandBar and the Waterfront.

877 N Shore Dr.
Anna Maria, Florida 34216

rodreelresort.com

Top left: Courtesy of Digital Commonwealth. *Top right and bottom*: Courtesy of Rod and Reel Resort

Bon-Aire Resort

St. Pete Beach

Opened: 1953 | Rooms: 80

What makes it special: The giant neon Bon-Aire sign is a Gulf Boulevard landmark.

In 1952, Chicagoans William and Gladys Curotto bought land on St. Pete Beach and started building a 16-room motel. They named it in honor of the fresh sea air the spot enjoyed: Bon-Aire. Over time, the Curottos continued adding to the property, increasing it up to 60 rooms by 1969. When William died that spring, he left the business to his children, William Jr. and Carol Ann Upham. That winter, the family bought a neighboring motel, El-Jomar, and continued expanding. The property's neon Bon-Aire sign is an iconic part of Gulf Boulevard, and in 2017, it became a historic landmark. Today, many of the Bon-Aire's guests are third- and fourth-generation visitors, returning with their grandchildren to the place their own grandparents brought them on vacation. The resort includes two swimming pools, shuffleboard courts, beach views, and Sandbar Bill's, a beachfront restaurant.

If you visit: Make a reservation for Spinners Rooftop Grille just down the street at the top of the Bellwether Beach Resort. This spot for fine dining sits on the hotel's 12th floor and slowly spins, offering 360-degree views of the beach and the bay while you dine.

4350 Gulf Blvd.
St. Pete Beach, Florida 33706

bonaireresort.com

Top row and bottom right: Courtesy of Bon-Aire Resort
Middle: Courtesy of Kristen Hare. *Bottom left:* Courtesy of State Library and Archives of Florida

Bon-Aire

THE VAGABOND HOTEL

MIAMI

OPENED: 1953 | ROOMS: 42

WHAT MAKES IT SPECIAL: THIS JET-AGE MOTEL HELPED DEFINE MIAMI'S BISCAYNE BOULEVARD, FIRST FOR GOOD, THEN BAD, AND NOW FOR GOOD AGAIN.

The Vagabond Motel opened on Miami's Biscayne Boulevard in 1953, designed by architect Robert Swartburg. It featured nude sea nymphs and neon shooting stars. Like other motels around it, the Vagabond was a hip spot until it and its neighborhood weren't. By the mid-1970s, business was bad, said the owner at the time in a *Miami Herald* article. "Even before people get to Miami, they are told to stay away from Biscayne Boulevard. People are afraid of being mugged or robbed if they stay here." When the Vagabond closed, it stayed that way, despite many efforts to revive it. According to the City of Miami: Historic Preservation, "This classic 'jet age' motel embodies the characteristics of the Miami Modern style, including an open-air plan, jalousie windows, geometric designs, overhanging roof lines, stone facing, and sculptural elements depicting marine life and other nautical themes." In 2013, developer Avra Jain bought the Vagabond and brought it back to life. It reopened in 2014 as the Vagabond Hotel. Now, the MiMo Biscayne Boulevard Historic District, which includes the Vagabond and the Selina Gold Dust, is once again a thriving spot.

IF YOU VISIT: THE MIAMI DESIGN PRESERVATION LEAGUE OFFERS AN ART DECO WALKING TOUR THAT HIGHLIGHTS THE MANY STYLES THAT MAKE UP THE CITY, INCLUDING MIMO.

7301 BISCAYNE BLVD.
MIAMI, FLORIDA 33138

thevagabondhotelmiami.com

Top right: Courtesy of State Library and Archives of Florida. *All others:* Courtesy of The Vagabond Hotel

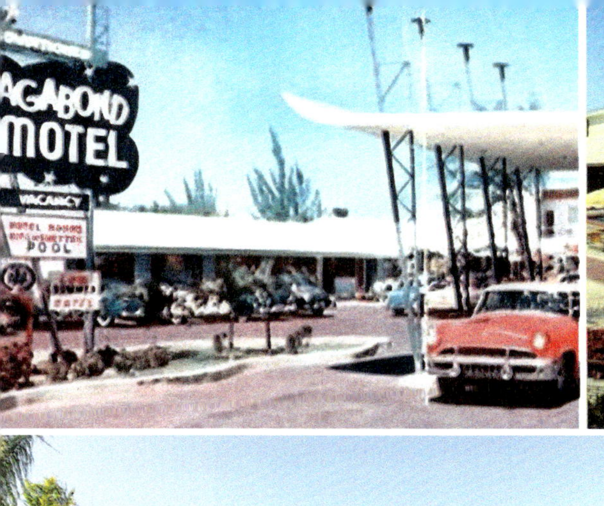

AGABOND
MOTEL
VACANCY
POOL

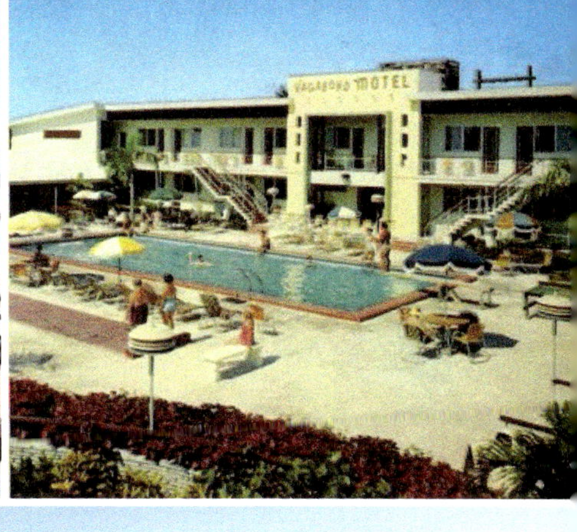

VAGABOND MOTEL

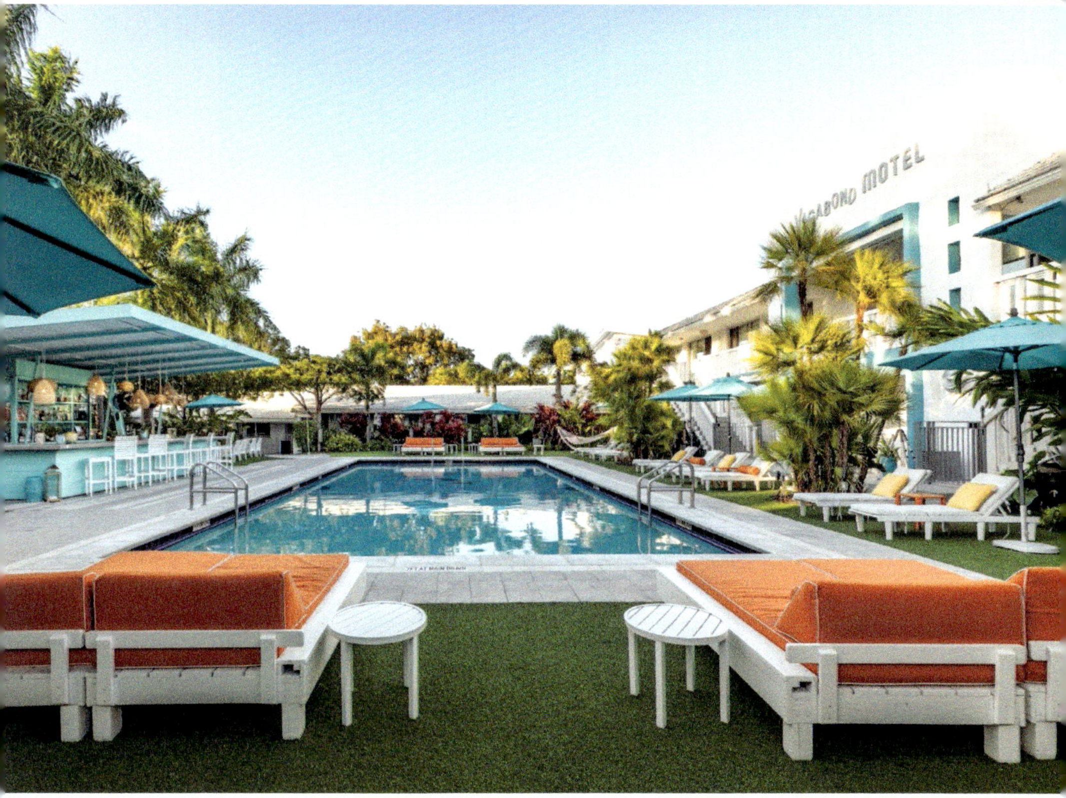
AGABOND MOTEL

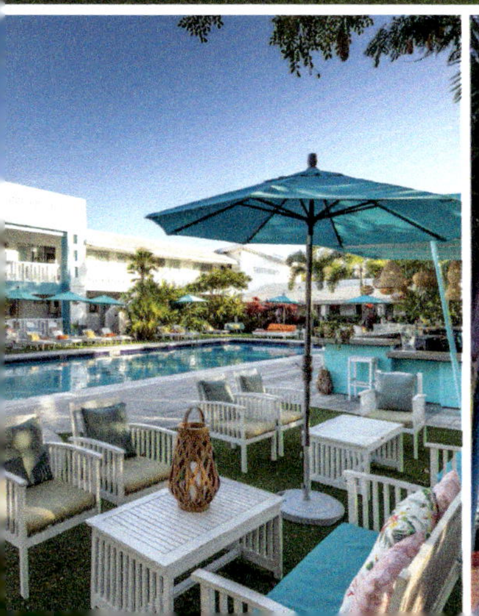

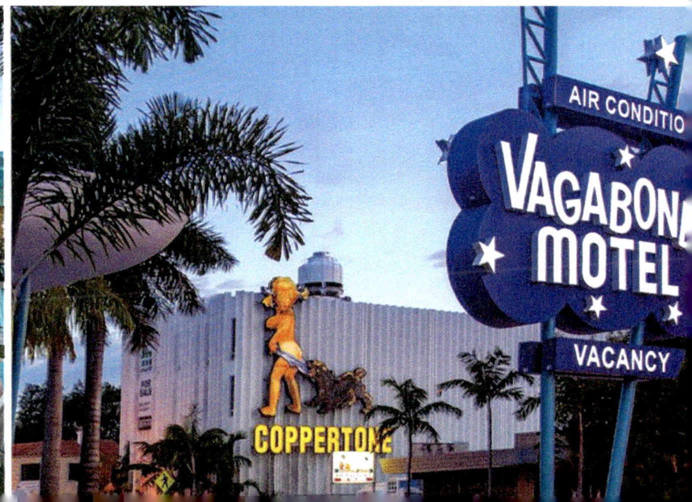

AIR CONDITIO
VAGABON
MOTEL
VACANCY
COPPERTONE

Eden Roc

Miami Beach

Opened: 1955 | Rooms: 415

What makes it special: The neon sign, the shape, the lobby, the location on Collins Avenue. Take your pick.

Miami in the 1950s was home to MiMo, or Miami Modern architecture, and Eden Roc was a prime example with influences from the Italian Renaissance. The hotel's owner, Harry Mufson, told architect Morris Lapidus to make sure it had "plenty of glamour, and make sure it screams luxury," according to the hotel. Named after another hotel on the French Riveria, Miami's version of the hotel opened in December of 1955 with performances by Harry Belafonte. The *Miami Herald* reported that the hotel brought many firsts to Miami Beach, including underground parking, a private yacht basin, "and an escalator going from the hotel to the swimming pool and cabana area." It also had a movie theater, five dining rooms, and a supper club. Eden Roc would host other great musicians, including Frank Sinatra and Sammy Davis Jr., and stars including Elizabeth Taylor. When it opened, the Eden Roc broke with the segregation of the time and allowed Black artists to stay there, according to the hotel. Visit today for stunning views in the circular lobby, art displays, and a glimpse of the hotel's iconic neon sign.

If you visit: Take the Jewish Miami Beach Tour from the Design Preservation League and learn about that community's pivotal role in shaping Miami Beach.

4525 Collins Ave.
Miami Beach, Florida 33140

edenrochotelmiami.com

Bottom left: Courtesy of State Library and Archives of Florida. *All others:* Courtesy of Eden Roc

B Ocean Resort

Fort Lauderdale

Opened: 1956 | Rooms: 484

What makes it special: There sure aren't a lot of hotels shaped like a ship.

"Six floors below the 'sun deck' of the Yankee Clipper hotel, now under construction on the south beach, will be a cocktail lounge called The Wreck," the *Fort Lauderdale News* reported in 1956. "It will have the appearance of a ship's hull resting on the ocean floor. Through windows on one side, human mermaids will be seen in the pool . . . " That summer, the hotel was ready to launch with those mermaids, a Polynesian dinner review, and a ship-shaped spot. In 1966, the hotel became part of the Sheraton hotel family. In 2005, it was sold to Starwood Capital Group. In 2010, it reopened as the Sheraton Ft. Lauderdale Beach Hotel. In 2015, it became the B Ocean Resort. Throughout changes in name and owners, a few things have remained here. It's still shaped like a ship. And the Wreck Bar still has mermaids. These days, they perform burlesque shows Thursdays, Fridays, and Saturdays, and there's a family-friendly brunch with the mermaids on Sundays.

If you visit: Mimosas and mermaids? What's not to love?!

1140 Seabreeze Blvd.
Fort Lauderdale, Florida 33316

boceanresort.com

Top right: Courtesy of Digital Commonwealth
All others: Courtesy of B Ocean Resort

Selina Miami Gold Dust

Miami

Opened: 1957 | Rooms: 57

What makes it special: Many of the motels in MiMo reflect 1950s modern architecture, but the Gold Dust is Miami's version of the Wild West.

"There's gold on the boulevard," the *Miami Herald* reported in the summer of 1957 when the ground was broken for architect Marcus Weintraub's Gold Dust Motel. Opening just a few years after the nearby Vagabond Motel, the Gold Dust joined what became "the motel capital of Miami" on Biscayne Boulevard, part of US Highway 1, which took motorists from Key West to Maine. "It guaranteed the Boulevard's strategic location as a place for motels catering to the automobile-borne tourist," according to a designation report from Miami's Historic Preservation Board. And the Gold Dust was guaranteed a prime spot on the boulevard thanks to a neighbor that moved in across the street in 1961, the Miami Playboy Club. But the glitter of that gold dust didn't last. By the 1970s, Biscayne Boulevard motels had become a seedy spot to spend an hour or two. In the early 2000s, a developer bought the motel and attempted to clean it up, raising rates from around $30 to $48 a night, the *Miami Herald* reported. The Gold Dust found the prospector it needed in 2018 with developer Avra Jain,

who also renovated the Vagabond. In 2021, the hotel reopened as the Selina Miami Gold Dust, a hotel and coworking space run by the Latin American hotel group. Biscayne Boulevard isn't the motel capital of Miami anymore, but it is now the MiMo Biscayne Boulevard Historic District. "The buildings constructed along this wide corridor illustrate Miami's changing fortunes," read the historic district's designation report. Thanks to spots like the Gold Dust, those fortunes are looking up again.

IF YOU VISIT: SEE ANOTHER MIMO MARVEL, THE BISCAYNE HOTEL, AND GRAB DELICIOUS COMFORT FOOD AT THE HOTEL'S RESTAURANT, BLUE COLLAR.

7700 BISCAYNE BLVD.
MIAMI, FLORIDA 33138

selina.com/usa/miami-gold-dust

Courtesy of Selina Miami Gold Dust

Thunderbird Beach Resort

Treasure Island

Opened: 1958 | Rooms: 106

What makes it special: The hotel's giant neon Thunderbird sign is a landmark on Treasure Island.

The Thunderbird almost wasn't the Thunderbird at all. When construction began on it in 1957, the owners of a Miami Beach Thunderbird Motel weren't too happy. A lawsuit followed against builders Thomas and Hazel King. The lawsuit continued for months, but ultimately a judge ruled the Treasure Island Thunderbird could keep its name. Soon, the Thunderbird was making news for full rooms, happy tourists, and beachy gimmicks. "Found a real shrunken head," read a 1959 classified ad that ran regularly. "Come and see it at the Headhunter's Lounge at the Thunderbird Motel, Treasure Island." In 1999, the giant Thunderbird lost its 2,000 bulbs in favor of neon lighting, according to reporting from the *St. Petersburg Times.* The King family owned the Thunderbird and sold the hotel in 2021. Today, the famous thunderbird still sits on a five-story pylon looking out on Gulf Boulevard. If you visit, there's one more Thunderbird to see—it's made of tile and rests at the bottom of the swimming pool.

If you visit: Journey into St. Petersburg to see another roadside attraction, Sunken Gardens. This spot is an oasis now surrounded by city with its own flamboyance of flamingos.

10700 Gulf Blvd.
Treasure Island, Florida 33706

thunderbirdflorida.com

Top photo by Kristen Hare. *Bottom left:* Courtesy of Barbara Driscoll, president, Treasure Island Historical Society. *Bottom right:* Courtesy of State Library and Archives of Florida

Warm Mineral Springs Motel

Warm Mineral Springs

Opened: 1958 | Rooms: 29

What makes it special: Built to mimic fountains, the architecture of this motel is still a showstopper.

Since the 1950s, people have come from around the world to soak in the prehistoric waters of Warm Mineral Springs. In March of 1958, they came for a new motel. "Estimated 10,000 people attended the open house staged Sunday by Warm Mineral Springs Motel, resulting in the largest traffic jam ever recorded in the southern end of Sarasota County," the *Bradenton Herald* reported. They came in those record-breaking numbers to see the "ultramodern" design of Sarasota architect Victor Lundy. Using hyperbolic paraboloids, Lundy built the motel to look like a series of fountains in homage to the springs, once thought to be the fountain of youth. "The motel's unique mushroom Champagne glass style roof with its glass walls enabled the residents to look at the stars from their beds at night . . . ," the motel's website explains. Built in an L shape originally, it later got additions that turned it into a U shape and a pool was added. Today, the motel's lobby still features the original curved wooden reception desk. And though development has happened all around the motel, its singular design still stands out.

If you visit: Go soak in Warm Mineral Springs. It's not the fountain of youth, but all those minerals will make you feel good.

12597 S Tamiami Trl.
Warm Mineral Springs, Florida 34287

warmmineralspringsmotel.com

Top left and right: Courtesy of State Library and Archives of Florida. *Middle, bottom left and right:* Courtesy of Kristen Hare

WARM
MINERAL SPRINGS

Sunset Inn & Cottages

Treasure Island

Opened: 1950s | Rooms: six motel rooms, six cottages, and one penthouse

What makes it special: Originally the Coral Lee, this bright spot is now a modern wink at the mid-century.

The Coral Lee, built in the futuristic, 1950s space-age Googie style, is one spot that's returned to its roots. The six-room motel opened in the 1950s and expanded to include the six cottages next door. Ownership and the property's name changed over time, and the spot went through a revival after new owners, Verdigreen, took over in 2022. The Sunset Inn and Cottages now feel classic in the most modern ways, with a space-age makeover that winks at the past. One of the cottages continues the original Coral Lee's legacy, too. Painted coral, of course, it was renamed Coral Lee and displays the original motel's logo on an outside mural. Inside, original brochures and postcards are on display. "A pretty picture," an early motel brochure reads. "Coral Lee is situated on the southernmost end of Treasure Island with the white sand shores of the Gulf of Mexico on one side and the quiet waters of Boca Ciega Bay on the other. Coral Lee is one of those treasured spots you must 'discover.'"

If you visit: Stop by the Florida Shell Shop on Gulf Boulevard. While you can always find beautiful shells at the actual beach, this is a spot for excellent shell hunting that's been around since 1955.

7925 W Gulf Blvd.
Treasure Island, Florida 33706

sunsetinnti.com

Top left: Courtesy of Barbara Driscoll, president, Treasure Island Historical Society
Other photos: Courtesy of Sunset Inn

STOP
7925

1960s

AND

1970s

Railroad magnates Henry Plant and Henry Flagler established the idea of Florida tourism. Walt Disney reinvented it.

"Walt Disney changed the paradigm for the rest of the 20th century," said historian Joseph Vars.

Florida wasn't just a naturally exotic place anymore, it was a place that could be futuristic. Or foreign. Or whatever else visitors desired.

"Florida's this blank slate," said historian Rodney Kite-Powell, "and Disney took full advantage of this blank slate to crate this image of Florida."

The growth in franchise motels, including Howard Johnsons, Days Inn and Holiday Inn, led to another change during this time, said Historic Hotels of America's Lawrence Horwitz—those chains led the way for desegregation.

There were cruel and violent times to come in this era, too, including the 1964 swim-in at a White St. Augustine motor lodge that ended when the owner poured acid into the water. The very next day, the Civil Rights Act of 1964 was approved.

Bilmar Beach Resort

Treasure Island

Opened: 1961 | Rooms: 167

What makes it special: Bilmar was named after the children of the couple who built it, Bill and Margot.

When the Bilmar Beach Resort opened on Treasure Island in December of 1961, it was the first luxury resort built there in years, the press reported. It drew tourists and locals from its prime spot on the Gulf of Mexico, a sparkling pool, sundeck, and regular fashion shows. Rooms touted air-conditioning, telephones, and televisions. "Tiny flowering plants in small clay pots that permit guests to take them home as souvenirs are being recommended by smart decorators for use as placecards at dinner parties," the press reported at the time. The BilMar, as it was known in its early days, was built by Russell and Connie Baltz. The couple named the motel after their children, Bill and Margot. They opened another BilMar in Grand Haven, Michigan. The Bilmar expanded into three buildings with two pools over the years. It was sold by Bill Baltz in 2000 and has had different ownership over the years. It now includes the restaurant Sloppy Joe's on the Beach. Bilmar regulars include Kim and Denise, two employees who've worked there for more than 30 years, and four generations of one family that have visited for the Fourth of July since the 1960s. The hotel was renovated in 2018 and today has a chic retro feel.

If you visit: Behold the stunning sandcastles at the annual Sanding Ovations Master Cup, which takes place each fall on the beach behind the Bilmar.

10650 Gulf Blvd.
Treasure Island, Florida 33706

bilmarbeachresort.com

Courtesy of Bilmar Beach Resort

Disney's Polynesian Village Resort

Lake Buena Vista

Opened: 1971 | Rooms: 400-plus

What makes it special: Visiting this Disney resort can feel like a tiny bit of international travel in Florida.

When Disney's Polynesian-themed resort opened in 1971, it featured a lobby waterfall, luaus, and fire dancing, according to *Walt Disney World Magazine*. The Disney resort took what tourists and developers had been cultivating in Florida for decades—escapism—and made it international. "Architecturally resembling a royal Tahitian assembly lodge, the hotel's landmark is the Great Ceremonial House," the *Orlando Sentinel* reported that year. "Its open lobby, offices, shops and meeting rooms surround a central atrium with towering palm trees and cascading waterfalls. Natural sunlight comes in through a third-story skylight, topped by a peaked roof of massive Tahitian timber beams." The Polynesian Revue was performed here until 2003. The South Pacific–inspired resort, on the shores of the man-made Seven Seas Lagoon, has been renovated over the years and now includes nods to *Moana*. Activities at the resort these days include boat rentals, fishing, and an electrical water pageant.

If you visit: Trader Sam's Grog Grotto and Tiki Bar is tough to get into, but if you can find a spot at this tiny bar, it's worth the wait.

1600 Seven Seas Dr.
Lake Buena Vista, Florida 32830

disneyworld.disney.go.com/resorts/polynesian-resort

Top, middle and bottom right: Courtesy of Kristen Hare. *Bottom left:* Courtesy of State Library and Archives of Florida, 1981

Disney's Contemporary Resort

Lake Buena Vista

Opened: 1971 | Rooms: 500-plus

What makes it special: The nine-story mural inside the hotel was created by the same artist behind *Cinderella, Alice in Wonderland* and *Peter Pan.*

In the early 1970s, Walt Disney was nearing completion of a new theme park in central Florida, "and the best symbol of that is the 'contemporary resort hotel' now taking shape a few hundred yards from the castle on the shores of Bay Lake," the *St. Petersburg Times* reported in the spring of 1971. The concept: a 14-story A-frame hotel with a hollow interior where an electric monorail train would pass through every few minutes. According to *Walt Disney World Magazine,* the hotel was built using the architecture of a cruise ship. The interior features a nine-story *Grand Canyon* mural by Disney artist Mary Blair. Blair was also a lead designer for Disney's "It's a Small World." The hotel has been updated since opening, with different spots to eat and drink, including the rooftop California Grill, which offers epic views from the top of an epic spot.

If you visit: You don't have to stay at a Disney resort to enjoy the Disney resorts. Try a resort bar hop using the monorail and visit the bars at the Contemporary, the Polynesian, and the Grand Floridian.

4600 N World Dr.
Lake Buena Vista, Florida 32830

disneyworld.disney.go.com/resorts/contemporary-resort

Top, middle and bottom right: Courtesy of State Library and Archives of Florida
Bottom left: Courtesy of Kristen Hare

TAMPA AIRPORT MARRIOTT

TAMPA

OPENED: 1973 | ROOMS: 298

WHAT MAKES IT SPECIAL: IF YOU HAVE TO STAY AT AN AIRPORT, THIS IS THE WAY TO DO IT.

In 1971, the *Tampa Tribune* wrote about "Tampa's new crown jewel." "Paris has a tower, London has a palace, and New York has a certain skyscraper. Visitors are expected to see these landmarks . . . Tampa now has its new air terminal." Among the things making the airport so epic? The airport's Host International Hotel, which featured a revolving restaurant. The hotel opened two years later, in 1973. The ballroom included a chandelier with 2,712 light bulbs. In 1981, Marriott bought Host International and its properties, including the Tampa Airport hotel. It's been the owner since. In 2013, the revolving restaurant, the View at CK's, closed. For its 50th anniversary in 2022, the hotel got a modern makeover. The rotating restaurant is still closed, but it is available for events.

IF YOU VISIT: MAKE SURE TO GO AND VISIT PHOEBE, THE 21-FOOT FLAMINGO ART INSTALLATION YOU CAN FIND IN THE AIRPORT'S MAIN TERMINAL.

4200 GEORGE J. BEAN PKWY.
TAMPA, FLORIDA 33607

marriott.com

Top, middle and bottom right: Courtesy of State Library and Archives of Florida. *Bottom left:* Courtesy of Marriott International

FLORIDA'S HISTORIC BLACK-OWNED HOTELS, MOTELS, AND INNS

As both tourism boomed in Florida and the many people and institutions upholding segregation settled in, hotels where Black travelers could stay grew in number. Many were listed in the *Green Book,* a guide to help Black motorists navigate the country.

"So in a sense, these hotels provided a refuge for people," said Marvin Dunn, a professor emeritus of psychology at Florida International University and the creator of Dunn Tours, which highlights Black history in Miami. "They served a purpose beyond just comfort. They were a place of safety."

They were also places for joy—wedding teas and ladies' lunches, beauty pageants, pool parties, and nights out with the biggest artists at iconic nightclubs. And they were places where Black entrepreneurs found success.

In Plant City, Janie Wheeler Bing was one of them. "This was a woman, a Black woman in the 1920s, who, as the kids say, ran a side hustle," said William Thomas Jr., president of the Improvement League of Plant City, which now owns and runs the Bing Rooming House Museum. "She was a teacher and wanted to run a hotel business out of her home."

In Orlando, Henry Sadler ran his own hotel while continuing to work for other hotels in the area. And in Miami, Georgette Scott Campbell created a tearoom and rooming house where Billie Holiday was a frequent guest. Their stories show how people overcame both stereotypes and the environment, Thomas said. It's not a side of Black history that most people are used to seeing, Dunn said. But it happened and this is what it looked like.

The Jackson House

Tampa

Opened: 1910 | Rooms: 206

What made it special: Until his death, the original owners' grandson worked to preserve the Jackson House's history. Now, people in Tampa continue the work.

Moses Jackson built his family home in Tampa's Scrub neighborhood, and thanks to its proximity to the Union Station Train Depot, according to reporting from the *Tampa Bay Times,* he soon saw an opportunity. In 1910, he and his wife, Sarah, opened their home to guests, including the musicians traveling the country who weren't allowed to stay at other hotels because of segregation. When he died, his wife took over. She also ran Jackson Cab Co., then Tampa's only Black-owned cab service, the *Tampa Tribune* reported. When Sarah Jackson died in 1937, her daughters, Ora Dee, Josephine, and then Alberta took over running the property over the years. In 1940, the job fell to the youngest daughter, Sarah Jackson Robinson. In 2011, her son Willie Robinson Jr. started a restoration effort and a foundation one year later, which is still working to preserve the space. "I look at this house, and it's a house," he told the *Tampa Tribune* at the time, "but it's a symbol of what hard work and what a family can do."

If you visit: Student groups can work with the Tampa Bay History Center and take the Central Avenue Black History Walking Tour, which includes the Jackson House.

851 E Zack St.
Tampa, Florida 33602

jacksonhousfoundation.org

Top left: Courtesy of Tampa Bay History Center. *Top right, middle, and bottom:* Courtesy of Tampa-Hillsborough County Public Library System. *Bottom left:* Courtesy of Kristen Hare

Mary Elizabeth Hotel

Miami

OPENED: 1921 | CLOSED: 1983

WHAT MADE IT SPECIAL: THIS HOTEL WAS RUN BY A BUSINESSWOMAN IN A TIME WHEN WOMEN WEREN'T ALLOWED TO DO MUCH BUSINESS.

In 1921, Dr. William B. Sawyer built the Mary Elizabeth Hotel in Miami, and his wife, Alberta Sawyer, ran it, according to the Black Archives History and Research Foundation of South Florida. The Mary Elizabeth sat at 642 Northwest Second Avenue in Miami's Overton neighborhood. It had 37 rooms and two lounges, the Flamingo Room and the Zebra Lounge. "Miami's Mary Elizabeth Hotel finest in south," read a headline from the *Miami Times* in 1948, with the subhead "swanky hotel rates with best." "New York has Theresa and Detroit has its Gotham," the article reported, but the finest hotel in the South for Black travelers was the Mary Elizabeth. The hotel hosted Latin Americans traveling in Miami and had a penthouse with a roof garden and a "compact but classy cocktail lounge which serves as a mecca for the social elite." Guests over the years included W. E. B. DuBois, Thurgood Marshall, and Bessie Smith. Overton was a thriving Black hub until 1956, according to the University of Miami Libraries, when the city built the Miami Expressway right through the middle of the neighborhood. After a few difficult decades, the Mary Elizabeth was demolished in 1983. It is today recognized as a lost landmark in one of Miami's once-thriving communities.

IF YOU VISIT: MAKE TIME TO EXPLORE THE BLACK ARCHIVES AT THE NEARBY HISTORIC LYRIC THEATER IN OVERTON. THIS 1913 THEATER ONCE HOSTED LEGENDARY PERFORMERS.

Season's Greetings

OM THE STAFF OF THE MARY ELIZABETH HOTE

Courtesy of *Miami Times*, 1951 and 1952

The Jolliettes Social Club

PROUDLY PRESENTS ITS

WEEKLY JAM SESSIONS

AT THE BEAUTIFUL

FLAMINGO ROOM

MARY ELIZABETH HOTEL

Every Sunday

5 'til 9 P.M.

Admission 60c tax incl.

TABLES FREE

DRESS COOL — COME AND ENJOY YOURSELF

Bing Rooming House

Plant City

Opened: 1928 | Closed: 1975

What made it special: The Bing was an anchor for Plant City's Black business district.

The Bing Rooming House on Laura Street in Plant City anchored the African American business district, according to the museum, and it gave its proprietress, Janie Wheeler Bing, extra income. Bing was a teacher, and the rooming house and restaurant next door allowed her and her husband to care for their family while hosting guests and customers. The Bing was one of the few Black businesses in Plant City with a telephone. Old guest logs show that baseball players Jackie Robinson and Satchel Paige stayed there while playing in the Negro League. The Bing closed in 1975, and Mrs. Bing died in 1984. In 1995, her grandson, James "Jimmy" Washington deeded the property to the Improvement League of Plant City, a nonprofit. And soon they started working to preserve it. That work included lifting the second floor of the house up on stilts, adding a concrete slab on the first floor, and replacing the wood in the walls there piece by piece.

If you visit: The Bing Rooming House Museum is open Wednesdays, Thursdays, and Fridays for a deeper dive into history.

205 S Allen St.
Plant City, Florida 33563

plantcitybinghouse.com

Courtesy of Improvement League of Plant City

Rogers Hotel

Tampa

OPENED: 1940 | CLOSED: THE BUILDING BURNED DOWN IN 1974

WHAT MADE IT SPECIAL: G.D. ROGERS WAS A SELF-MADE BUSINESSMAN AND PHILANTHROPIST.

G. D. Rogers came to Florida from Georgia with nothing, according to Friends of the Tampa River Walk. By 1922, he helped start the Central Life Insurance Company to sell policies to Black consumers. In 1940, Rogers bought the Central Hotel and started renovations. He went on to open the Rogers Hotel and the Rogers Dining Room on Tampa's Central Avenue. The hotel hosted conventions for Black businessmen and professionals and housed Negro League baseball players. In 1945, Rogers sold the hotel for $45,000, according to reporting from the *Tampa Tribune,* and it was renamed the Pyramid Hotel. Rogers continued making Tampa better, contributing to the formation of Rogers Park, the only spot where Black residents could picnic at the time. He died in 1951, at 66, and was memorialized in his short obituary for making Tampa a better place. He's remembered for just that today on Tampa's Historical Monument Trail on the city's Riverwalk.

IF YOU VISIT: GO SEE G. D. ROGERS'S BUST ON THE RIVERWALK AND MEET OTHER TAMPA LEGENDS ON THE HISTORICAL MONUMENT TRAIL, INCLUDING VICTORIANO MANTEIGA, THE FOUNDER OF TAMPA'S TRILINGUAL *LA GACETA* NEWSPAPER, AND BLANCHE ARMWOOD, WHO CHAMPIONED HOME ECONOMICS FOR BLACK STUDENTS AND LATER EARNED A LAW DEGREE.

Courtesy of Tampa-Hillsborough County Public Library System

NOTARY PUBLIC
O. D. ROGERS

GEORGETTE'S TEA ROOM HOUSE

MIAMI

OPENED: 1940 | CLOSED: EARLY 1960S

WHAT MADE IT SPECIAL: THIS SPOT WAS THE SITE OF YEARS OF SWANKY CELEBRATIONS.

In 1940, Georgette Scott Campbell opened a tearoom and rooming house that would come to be the setting for a few decades worth of celebrations. Georgette's Tea Room, on Northwest 51st Street in Miami, occupied a two-story, 13-room property. Scott Campbell had previously opened a tearoom in Harlem, according to reporting from the *New Tropic,* before returning to Miami to set up her new business. In stories over the years, the *Miami Times* called the spot "ultra swank," "fashionable," and a place of "fellowship and sisterhood." The hostess made news herself in the summer of 1955 when she wrote the *Miami Times* from Asbury Park "that she is having a restful vacation. She spent several days in Georgia, South Carolina and Baltimore, will complete a week's stay at Asbury Park and then at least 10 days at Saratoga, New York." Along with social events, Georgette's also hosted Black artists and entertainers including Billie Holiday. Georgette Scott Campbell died in 1962, and the house got historical designation in 1990, according to the *New Tropic.* It later became a residential home. Today, the property is owned by Bethany Seventh Day Adventist Church, which is working to renovate and preserve what Georgette Scott Campbell once made so special.

IF YOU VISIT: HEAD TO CALLE OCHO, SOUTHWEST EIGHTH STREET IN MIAMI'S LITTLE HAVANA NEIGHBORHOOD, AND EXPLORE ANOTHER COMMUNITY WITH DEEP ROOTS IN THE CITY.

2540 NW 51ST ST.
MIAMI, FLORIDA 33082

georgettestearoom.com

Top: Courtesy of State Library and Archives of Florida. *Bottom:* Courtesy of Georgette's Tea Room House

TOOKES HOTEL

TALLAHASSEE

OPENED: 1948 | CLOSED: 1980s

WHAT MADE IT SPECIAL: HOTEL OWNER DOROTHY NASH TOOKES ALSO HELPED ESTABLISH A SCHOOL FOR BLACK CHILDREN IN HER NEIGHBORHOOD.

In 1948, Dorothy Nash Tookes modified her home in Tallahassee's Frenchtown neighborhood and officially opened Tookes Rooming House, according to the registration form for the hotel's national historic designation. Tookes, a nurse and teacher, and her husband, a chef, converted their home into a hotel in the early 1950s, adding a neon sign out front in 1952. "Hotel records reflect the names of a couple of notable African Americans who stayed there, James Baldwin and Lou Rawls," according to the report. The Tookes continued expanding and hosting guests through the 1980s, the *Tallahassee Democrat* reported. In 1993, the hotel became Tookes Villa, a home for the elderly and mentally disabled. It later became a state halfway house. The spot went through renovations in the last several years, and in the summer of 2024, it was set to welcome guests again as an Airbnb.

IF YOU VISIT: WALK THE FRENCHTOWN HISTORICAL MARKER TRAIL AND LEARN ABOUT THE PEOPLE AND BUSINESSES OF ONE OF TALLAHASSEE'S PIONEERING BLACK COMMUNITIES.

Courtesy of State Library and Archives of Florida

Sir John Hotel

Miami

Opened: 1951 | Closed: 1976

What made it special: The iconic photo of Muhammad Ali shadowboxing underwater was taken in the pool of this once-iconic hotel.

The luxury Lord Calvert Hotel opened in Miami's bustling Overton neighborhood in 1951. "It has 118 rooms and includes a swimming pool, solarium and roof garden for dancing," the *Miami Times* reported. The hotel's nightclub and its pool were both hot spots. In 1956, the *Miami News* reported that the Lord Calvert had changed its name to Sir John Schenley, then quickly shortened it to Sir John. "The Knight Beat was an essential stop on the Chitlin Circuit, the parallel music world that many Black artists traveled in the days of segregation," the nonprofit Going Overton wrote. "The hotel's bustling pool was a popular hangout for visiting artists and prominent Black leaders, and the scene of Muhammad Ali's most famous posed photo." Entertainers at Knight Beat included Dinah Washington, Sam Cooke, Dick Gregory, Billie Holiday, and Mary Wells. When in Miami, Ali worked out in the empty nightclub during the day, the *Miami News* reported at the time. In 1976, the federal government bought the hotel and demolished it, putting a post office in its place, according to reporting from the *Miami Times*.

If you visit: Stop by Historic Virginia Key Beach Park, a spot where Black Miamians could enjoy the beach during segregation.

Courtesy of State Library and Archives of Florida

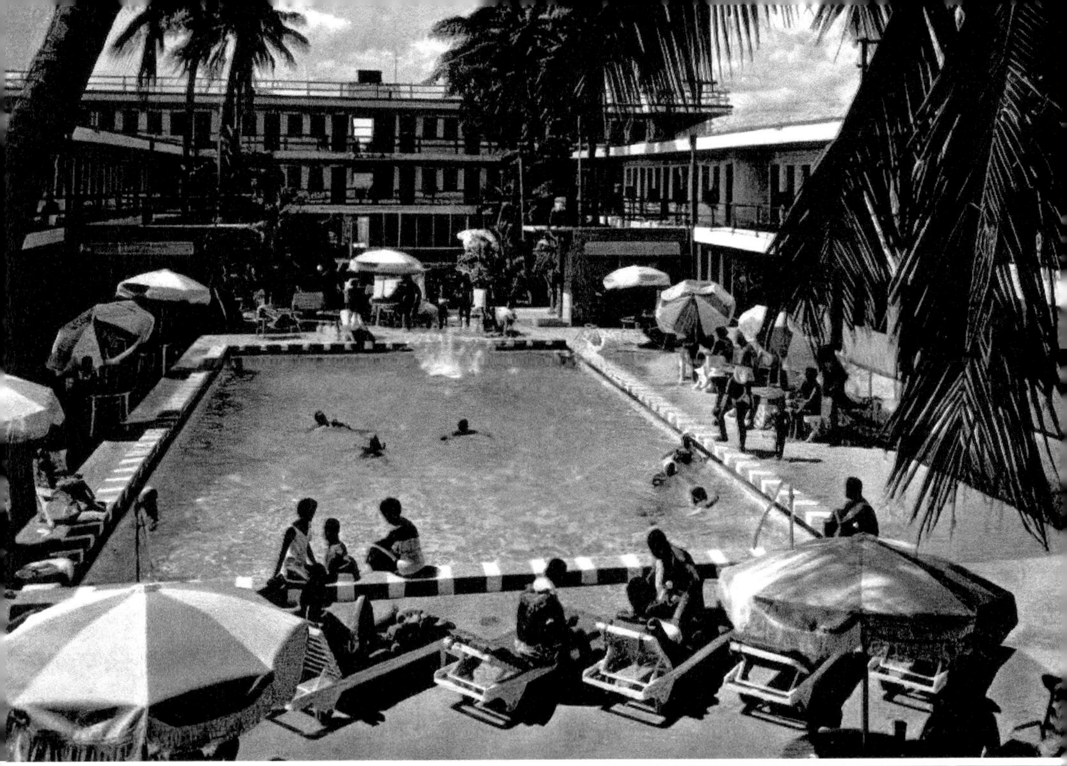

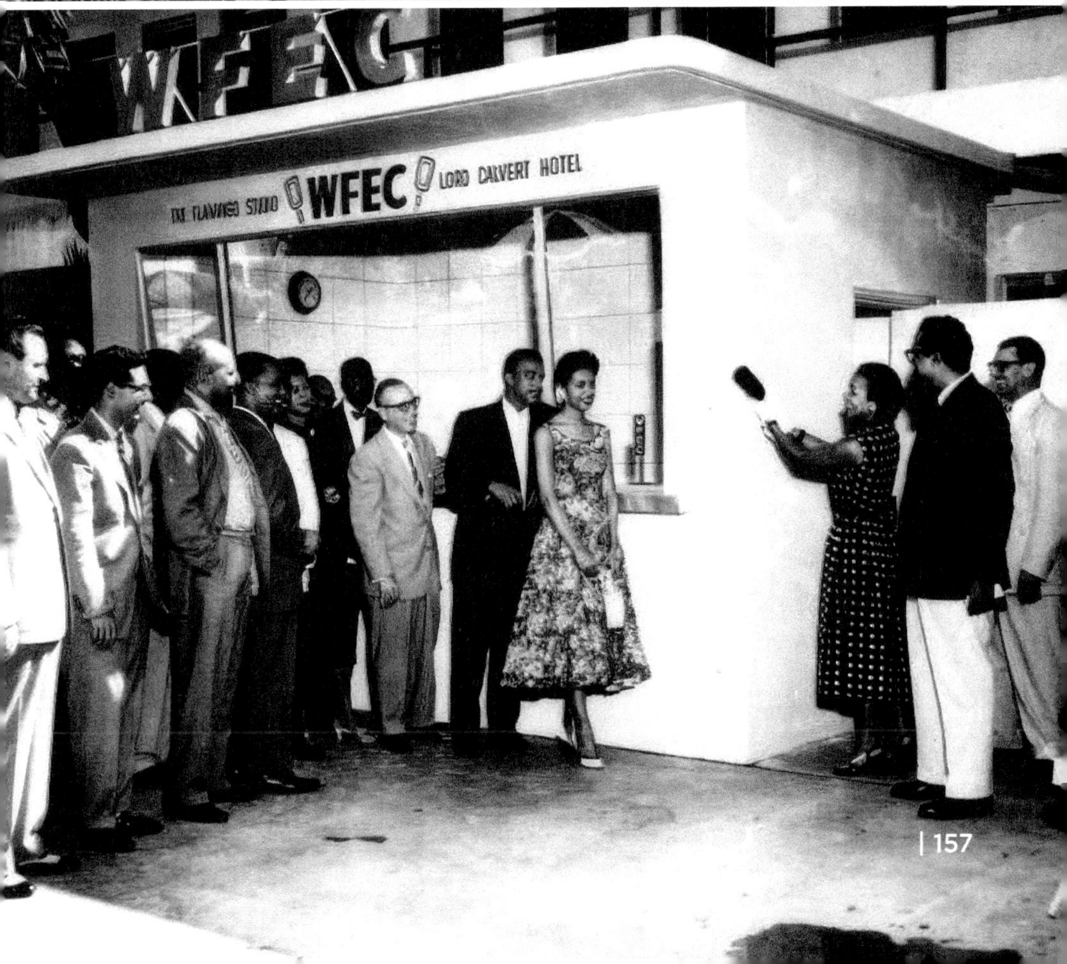
WFEC
THE FLAMINGO STUDIO
WFEC
LORD CALVERT HOTEL

HAMPTON HOUSE

MIAMI

OPENED: 1954 | CLOSED: 1976

WHAT MADE IT SPECIAL: IT'S STILL SPECIAL. THE COMMUNITY HAS REVIVED THIS ONCE-THRIVING AND ESSENTIAL SPOT IN AMERICAN CULTURE. IT'S NOW A MUSEUM AND VENUE.

In the summer of 1954, a new million-dollar, 50-room luxury motel opened in Miami with a ribbon cutting from Miami's mayor and 1,000 people in attendance, the *Miami Herald* reported at the time. The Booker Terraces, or the Booker T. as it came to be known, were soon advertising weekend getaways in "Miami's newest, Florida's finest . . . Swim in our filtered pool. Enjoy the South's finest cocktail lounge." In 1960, Harry and Florence Markowitz renovated the hotel and renamed it the Hampton House and Villas. It quickly became a cultural hub. Among the famous guests were Muhammad Ali, Jackie Robinson, Malcolm X, tennis player Althea Gibson, and, on several occasions, Martin Luther King Jr., who is reported to have honed his "I Have a Dream" speech while visiting the motel. The Hampton House is also the setting for the film "One Night in Miami," which imagines icons from the Civil Rights era gathering to talk about the movement. According to the Historic Hampton House, the Civil Rights Act of 1968 opened up housing and entertainment options for people of color and the community, and the motel struggled. It closed in 1976. In 2002, the community worked to save the building from demolition, and in 2015, the Historic Hampton House Community Trust began $6 million in restorations. The spot today is the Historic Hampton House Museum of Culture and Art.

IF YOU VISIT: THIS IS ONE OF THE FEW SPOTS ON THIS LIST YOU CAN ACTUALLY VISIT. SEE HOW THE ONCE-CENTRAL MOTEL HAS PRESERVED ITS PAST AS IT EXPLORES THE FUTURE.

4240 NW 27TH AVE.
MIAMI, FLORIDA 33142

historichamptonhouse.org

Courtesy of The Historic Hampton House

Hotel Sadler

Orlando

Opened: 1961 | Closed: 1989

What made it special: Henry Sadler was known at hotels around Orlando for excellent service.

"Henry Sadler, that fine bell captain at the San Juan hotel (for 35 years) is planning a hotel and office building on W. Church St. in the 600 block," the *Orlando Sentinel* reported in 1960. " . . . Financing hasn't been completed, but Henry says 'you ought to see the recommendations Orlando's three downtown banks gave me. I'm so proud I could bust.'" The Hotel Sadler opened at 619 West Church Street, according to the city of Orlando, in what was then a Black neighborhood. His two-story, 28-room hotel had a swimming pool and a coffee shop. The hotel hosted Black artists and athletes, including Ray Charles and James Brown. While he ran his own hotel, Sadler continued working as a bell captain at the San Juan until 1972, then he moved over to Howard Johnson's. "The first thing I do is learn a person's name so I can call him by his name the next time I see him," he told the *Orlando Sentinel* in 1977. "People like that. It gives them a good feeling. It gives me a good feeling." Sadler sold the Hotel Sadler in 1983 and went on to work in guest services at another Orlando hotel, the Court of Flags. The Sadler closed and was demolished in 1989. The devoted hotel man kept working, and the Court of Flags, which later became the Delta Orlando Resort, named a VIP suite after him.

If you visit: Stop by another historic Black hotel that's now a museum, the Wells'Built. Built by Dr. William Monroe Wells, this hotel also had a casino next door. Today it's the Wells'Built Museum of African American History and Culture.

Top: Courtesy of *Orlando Sentinel*. *Bottom:* Ad from *Orlando Sentinel*, 1961

A&M HOTEL

TALLAHASSEE

OPENED: 1962 | CLOSED: MID-1960S

WHAT MADE IT SPECIAL: THOUGH OPEN FOR A SHORT TIME, THIS FORMER HOSPITAL-TURNED-HOTEL HAD ALL THE MODERN AMENITIES.

The Tookes family of Tallahassee knew how to run a hotel by the 1960s. After more than 20 years running the Tookes Hotel, they started managing the brand-new A&M Hotel. It opened in 1961 in what had been the Laura Bell Memorial Hospital. "The establishment is fitted with wall-to-wall carpeting," read a story from the time. "There are upstairs and downstairs lobbies. A television set is located on the ground floor. Several bathing facilities are located on each floor. There is thermostat heat and air conditioning for year around comfort." The owner, W. H. Wilson, said at the time that Black travelers "need a first-class hotel when visiting here, and we have gone to great lengths to give it to them." By 1963, the *Tallahassee Democrat* reported, the Tookeses had leased the hotel from him and were running it. The hotel appears to have become student housing soon after.

IF YOU VISIT: YOU CAN ACTUALLY EXPLORE THIS ONE FROM HOME. HEAD TO THE FLORIDA CIVIL RIGHTS MUSEUM ONLINE AND LEARN ABOUT THE PEOPLE WHO WORKED AND FOUGHT FOR EQUALITY IN THE STATE, INCLUDING DOROTHY NASH TOOKES.

Courtesy of State Library and Archives of Florida

MODERN
MARVELS

Florida today has endless lodging options, from an old Chinook helicopter in Brooksville to a houseboat in Key West to a tree house in Kissimmee. There's a tiny house village in Matlacha, floating aqua lodges in Marathon, and multiple spots for glamping. Visit Florida Research reported that in 2023, the state had nearly 500,000 hotel and motel rooms at 4,659 properties. A few, unlike the rest of the properties in this book, are less than 50 years old. Still, they stand out and are worth appreciating.

Courtesy of Simonton Historic Inn and Cottages

Simonton Court Historic Inn & Cottages

Key West

Built in the 1880s, opened as a hotel in the 1980s

Rooms: 21 rooms, nine cottages

What makes it special: The inn's first life was as a cigar factory.

Ten different buildings make up Simonton Court Historic Inn & Cottages in Key West, and they're all classic Key West. The inn was originally a cigar factory, according to the property, and the nearby conch cottages were the homes of the factory's employees. The Simonton also includes a mansion, a townhouse, gardens, and four swimming pools. According to news clippings, the address was also once home to a seamstress and later a talented young pianist. Today, the hotel offers a three-hour Simonton Court food and history tour.

If you visit: Key West has a great selection of walking tours, from the Jimmy Buffett tours to ghost tours to pirate tours. These offer a great way to see a place while you poke around spots you might not have otherwise.

320 Simonton St.
Key West, Florida 33040

simontoncourt.com

Pyramids in Florida

Fort Myers

Opened: 2001 | Rooms: 26 pyramids

What makes it special: Egypt has the sphinx, and Florida's pyramids have a bust of Beethoven.

The Pyramids in Florida are among the youngest dwellings in this book, but their design is ancient. In 1997, two Austrians broke ground on a complex of pyramids on 11 acres in Fort Myers that they envisioned as winter retreats for Europeans. The design is the work of the late Walter Freller and his partner, homeopathic doctor Gerti Höntzsch, who set out to create an energy oasis. "Owners testify to a feeling of well-being inside the pyramids where the natural energy is concentrated by the shape of the building," the *News-Press* reported in 2002. Many of the pyramids sit around a thermal mineral lake. There's also massage, a barefoot path to activate reflexology, yoga, nordic walking, and an 11-acre Jungle Park for rambling. The 30-foot-tall Beethoven bust, at the entrance, was an early gift from the director of the Salzburg Festival and stands as an ode to joy and peace at the pyramids.

If you visit: See where the rich fellas kept warm at the Edison and Ford Winter Estates. While there, check out the Edison Botanic Research Laboratory, the only place in Florida designated as a National Historical Chemical Landmark.

7020 Constitution Loop
Fort Myers, Florida 33967

pyramidsinflorida.com

Courtesy of Pyramids in Florida

Courtesy of Kristen Hare

Le Méridien Tampa, The Courthouse

Tampa

Opened: Built in 1905, opened as a hotel in 2014 | Rooms: 130

What makes it special: Before it was a hotel, this grand building in Tampa's downtown was a federal courthouse. The judge's bench is now the front desk

This building in Tampa's downtown opened as an imposing federal courthouse in 1905. After decades spent working in that capacity and several years sitting empty, it became a grand hotel in 2014. Le Méridien Tampa, the Courthouse is full of old charm, including the witness stand, which is now the hostess stand at the hotel's restaurant, Sal Rosa; a golden eagle; and original wood paneling in the old courtroom and terrazzo marble throughout. The hotel's pool is the place where paddy wagons once pulled up with the accused. You can visit this hotel by eating at Sal Rosa or grabbing a drink at the hotel's bar or café. All three spots give a whole new twist to "order in the court."

If you visit: Check out another Tampa treasure at the nearby Tampa Theatre. This Florida Mediterranean movie palace is one of the few left in the state and features an ornate interior with electric stars that twinkle from the theater's sweeping ceiling.

601 N Florida Ave.
Tampa, Florida 33602

marriott.com

The Guitar Hotel at Seminole Hard Rock Hotel & Casino

Hollywood

Opened: 2019 | Rooms: 638

What makes it special: This giant guitar in the sky puts on a music and light show every night.

Paris has the Eiffel Tower. Las Vegas has the fountains of Bellagio. And South Florida has a giant guitar hotel that puts on a rocking show each night. The Guitar Hotel at the Seminole Hard Rock soars 450 feet into the sky with 2.3 million LED lights. It's the only guitar-shaped hotel in the world, and each night around 7, it puts on a show. The hotel has six beams of light that shoot out from the top like otherworldly guitar strings. During the day, it reflects the Florida sky, and at night, it lights up with music.

If you visit: You don't have to stay here to see the light show. Come by the casino or the Hard Rock Cafe, or just find a spot nearby around 7 on weeknights and 7 and 7:30 on weekends and wait to be dazzled.

1 Seminole Way
Hollywood, Florida 33314

seminolehardrockhollywood.com/hotel/the-guitar-hotel

Courtesy of Kristen Hare

Courtesy of Amelia Schoolhouse Inn

Amelia Schoolhouse Inn

Fernandina Beach

Opened: Built in 1886, opened as a hotel in 2019 | Rooms: 17

What makes it special: While nearly 50 years of learning took place here, today, it's a great place for exploring.

This schoolhouse was the first built on Amelia Island in 1886, according to the property. Today, it's a boutique hotel. The schoolhouse was designed by architect Robert Sands Schuyler. The community outgrew it by the 1930s, and it had several lives after, including as a library, offices, and Mason's Lodge. Today, it's a 17-room hotel with the schoolhouse's original staircase, windows, and heart pine floors carefully restored.

If you visit: You will not be sad to go to the Principal's Office because it's the hotel's bar. Order the Xtra Credit, which includes mezcal and mole bitters.

914 Atlantic Ave.
Fernandina Beach, Florida 32034

ameliaschoolhouseinn.com

Driftwood Hotel, Vero Beach: Courtesy of Digital Commonwealth

Courtesy of The Belleview Inn

APPENDIX

PANHANDLE AND NORTH FLORIDA

TAMPA BAY

Central Florida

South Florida

FLORIDA KEYS

MIAMI BILTMORE HOTEL AS SEEN FROM TARAGONA DR

PHOTO BY G. W. ROMER

AMI, FLORIDA.
60679
6
60679

The Don Ce-Sar, Pass-a-Grill Beach, courtesy of State Library and Archives of Florida

The Colony Hotel, Palm Beach, courtesy of Digital Commonwealth